THE PROMISE

God's Promise, Man's Obedience

By
Shanique Davis

Table of Content

ACKNOWLEDGEMENT

To my God and Father of my life, I thank you for this privilege to be called your child. I'm grateful for all that you did and all that you're about to me. I love you.

To my husband and confidant, thank you for being there for me through thick and thin. You have been a big help to me. I love you.

To all my friends, family, brother & sisters in Christ, and Pastor, you've all placed your part. May God be the rewarder of your labour, because it is certainly not in vain. I love you all.

PREFACE

Hebrews 10:23 & 35-36, KJV

[23] Let us hold fast the profession of our faith without wavering; (for he is faithful that promised;) [35] Cast not away therefore your confidence, which hath great recompense of reward. [36] For ye have need of patience, that, after ye have done the will of God, ye might receive the promise.

Writing this book was a challenge, primarily because I wrote it during one of the world's most dreaded crisis, COVID-19. My husband and I had random discussions about The Promise, long before we decided to write another book. I will never forget when I heard it as clear as day. We made records of what we thought were daily inspirations in our notepads, only to find out we had been writing another book- we only had to put it together.

God guided me by these words:

> "He that is faithful in a few things, continue so in it- the Lord will multiply it in due season. Remember, ye are lacking in nothing. Therefore, you MUST use what you have."

I was just as startled as I was thrilled that God made me this promise. I decided to dedicate these words of assurance that God spoke to me to all the mighty men and women of valour. Proverbs 15:23, KJV, says "A man hath joy by the answer of his mouth: and a word spoke in due season, how good it is!" The words He spoke are medicine, and He sent His word at the right time. My books were written and published with limited resources, and this confirmation guided me to completing many of my set goals during this season.

FOREWORD

The Promise: God's promise, Man's obedience is not a mere book but is a manifesto which speaks profoundly to God's promises to His people if we walk in obedience. The content is revelatory and inspirational. Mrs Shanique Davis has been given the mandate by Jesus Christ through the Holy Spirit to write this book which will bring about a great revelation of the promises of God through man's obedience. Her relationship with Jesus Christ emerged from a place of anguish, pain and brokenness. As a result of such, she developed this hunger and thirst for a more profound revelation and the actual manifestation of God's promises in her life. As she began to desire more of Jesus, she became aware of the fact that the promises of God are more attainable when she walks in obedience according to His words.

In scripture, the promise of God is the declaration or assurance given in His words of bestowing blessings on His people. Such confidence resting on the perfect justice, power, benevolence and immutable veracity of God cannot fail of performance. The Lord is not slack concerning His promises. (see 2 Peter 3). Obedience is the key that unlocks God's promises. In the word (bible), God links faith with obedience over and over. The promises of God are conditioned on you following the directions He gives. Deuteronomy 5:33 says follow all the instructions the Lord your God has given you, and life will go well for you.

God has made some incredible, specific promises in His words about obedience. Obedience is the premise behind all of the promises God gives you by Grace, but you get to enjoy His promises when you follow His instructions. Some of God's commands might sound confusing from the human perspective, but His word in Isaiah 55:8-9 speaks about His ways and thoughts are not ours but that they are higher.

I want you to enjoy all of God's promises. Obedience is the key that unlocks them. Choose to follow His directions today in faith. He promises to reward you for your obedience.

Mrs. Deneise Fearon

Minister/Prophetess

Author, "Faith in The Midst of Adversity: Inspirational Devotional" and Best Seller of "The Greater Call: My Encounter"

Certified International Life Coach and

Speaker.

deneisefearon@gmail.com

FOREWORD

Congratulations to Mrs. Shanique Davis on the achievement of this milestone – the completion of her second book. The title - *THE PROMISE: God's Promise, Man's Obedience* - explains how relevant to every human being is the subject dealt with in this book.

In the normal course of life, we make promises. Every person lives in expectancy of some kind. This book speaks to those experiences.

However, the author focusses on the faithfulness of God. God never fails to keep His word and promise. The strength of this book, I believe, lies in her practical but profound treatment of God's promises, and His ability to keep His word.

The definition of promise, and the several ways in which the author presents God's promises lay the foundation for the further treatment of the place of obedience.

This book, which is clearly born out of life's experiences, will certainly help others in their quest to follow the will and purpose of God for their lives.

It is an honour to be a part of Shanique's journey. I can testify to her desire and determination to be an inspiration to others. I commend this product as an easy-to-read, but meaningful companion text for all of us in our journey of life.

Congratulations again. "T.T."

Rev. Dr. Lenworth N. Anglin, C.D.
Pastor, Lecturer

INTRODUCTION

God has a grand plan for all of us, and until we get out of the way, we'll keep going around in circles. We must hold on to God's promises. You protect your promise when you are grounded in His Word. We know what God said, but we still have a responsibility, and that is to get ourselves in line to receive what the promise.

When the scripture says that man shall not live by bread alone (see Matthew 4:4), it means that God's word (command, divine instruction) can and will sustain you. God's word is truth; therefore, you need it to survive. His word keeps you connected to Him. God has promised in His word that He will save you, keep you, deliver you, and ensure all your daily needs met. *Cast not away, therefore, your confidence, which hath great recompense of reward. (See Hebrews 10:35, KJV)* Your trust in God is the object of your faith. God's promise is not magical or instantaneous. It comes through your obedience to divine instruction, love and faith in God, and a willingness to surrender your will for His. I.e., trust in God in every season of your life. Your promise is God's gift to you, and His investment in your life keeps you aligned with His will. Then, after you've done the will of God, through your obedience, faith and submission, you will receive His promise.

The Promise: God's Promise, Man's Obedience is compact with messages of God's promise and man's expectancy, addressed to the body of Christ, as well as those that are safe after they've done the will of God. These written messages were to highlight the mutual agreement between God and Man, and the importance of being obedient to God for you to receive your inheritance on this earth and the next life.

Living the life of fruitfulness and fulfilment is only possible after you've done the will of God. I.e., through your obedience, faith, and submission, you will receive your promise. Likewise, your disobedience can cause the delay in the fulfilment of the promises God made to you, and bridging that gap leads the way to what was promised and beyond.

Obedience is the condition on which God makes promises to man. God has made known this ruling since His first command to Adam (see Genesis 2:16-17). All that God has commanded you to do is to obey Him, and do it, so that you may live, be prosperous, and that you may inherit the blessing He has promised you. Live in expectancy for all that God has promised you.

My constant prayer for you is to walk in the blessings of your obedience, and that God's perfect vision for your life will become your most welcomed reality.

BE READY TO RECEIVE YOUR PROMISE…

WHAT IS A PROMISE?

A promise is an agreement that sets grounds for expectation. God's promise to us is an everlasting covenant that allows Him to bind Himself to man (see Deuteronomy 4:9; 6:7). He then honours His word and reinforces our trust in Him by being committed to what He said- so, He makes things happen. God's promise is His legally binding agreement with humanity (see Exodus 20; 31:18) that connects Heaven to Earth and transforms man's impossible to possible. When God gives us divine assurance, we expect that He will come through, no matter how long it takes (see Psalm 62:5).

In today's world, a promise carries much significance. A commitment in any form gives a person hope. It forms bonds and builds relationships of trust that can remain steady, healthy, and ever-growing for a lifetime. A promise leaves a lasting impact because of the expectation that follows that promise. It gives a sense of security and carries a mutual agreement between and among comrades. A promise keeper is a friend that is always in high demand. It is by far the best product ever made. Likewise, a broken promise carries the same potential to cause adverse devastation. A broken promise could break up friendships, families, marriages, churches, and even countries. When someone makes a promise and does not deliver, it's a disappointment that no one ever wants face. It is always best to say what you mean and only declare the things you are sure to achieve.

NEVER make promises you can't keep so that you can get someone to believe in you. No one looks for something they don't think will happen. They will one day see your halo was a rip-off, and you'll spoil your character.

Can you imagine if God were to dishonour His promises to you? What would happen if God hadn't meant what He said? Wouldn't it be right to say that God is a liar? God CANNOT lie, His word says it (see Numbers 23:19). The truth remains true only because God did what He said He would do. God's character is like no other. It is incomparable. God's promises are precious and pure (see Proverbs 10:22). No matter what your circumstances cause us to think or feel, God's promise to us still stands. God's promises are great and precious (see 2 Peter 1:4). God's promises are abundantly limitless and given to you through your obedience, faith, love, and submission to Him. God doesn't make promises lightly.

God's promise fuels you with the hope that in all your sufferings, trials, sicknesses, adverse chaos, loss, debt, and cares, He will see you through every bit of it. God will never tarnish His reputation by lying to you, or failing to deliver on His promise to you; He never forgets. God desires to have a close relationship with man, whether we think so or not. 1 John 4:19, KJV, says, "We love Him because He first loved us." He will do everything in His will to keep His promise, even if you don't keep yours, though you may forget. God always honours His word above His name. God is your Heavenly Father who promises that He'd never leave nor forsake you. He is the same yesterday, today, and forever, and there is no shadow of turning in Him.

God reinforces our trust in Him by staying committed to what He said. Since the beginning of time, God has been faithful. He is a Promise Keeping God (see Daniel 9:4). Why do you think He'd start lying now?

GOD'S PROMISE VS. MAN'S PROMISE

Genesis 29:15-27

Anyone can make promises, but not everyone will keep them. Has any man ever made you a commitment that they didn't keep? How many times have you heard, "I'll never do it again?" How many times have you heard, "I'll always be there when you need me?" What about that birthday gift, weekend getaway, a loan, or new accessory promised? Whatever it was, it must've set grounds for an expectation. The man who made you the promise probably forgot, maybe something important came up. I've heard those promises countless times, and I know and understand very well how disappointing it can be for someone to make a promise and not keep it. Just give them the benefit of the doubt- maybe it was just too good to be true. Hats off to all the persons who do their best to keep up with the promises they've made to others; I salute you!

Can you think of anyone who always keeps His promises? I can bet you already know the answer, but don't say it just yet. Let me tell you a story first.

Here is the story of man's promise.

A very long time ago in the land of Haran lived a man named Laban. He had two daughters, the eldest was called Leah, and the youngest was called Rachel. Laban's eldest daughter was cross-eyed, and his youngest daughter was fair and well-favoured. He had all that would make a man comfortable: sheep and cattle, herdsmen, wealth, and servants. One day, Laban's nephew, Jacob, was on a journey, as his mother had sent him to Laban to find a wife in her brother's house. When Jacob got the well (which was nearby), he asked the shepherds if they knew Laban and if he was well; they told him Laban was well and that his daughter, Rachel, was on her way to water the flock. Jacob greeted her and told her they were cousins, and Rachel went and told her father. Jacob was welcomed in their home and was staying with his relatives when Laban offered to pay Jacob for the work he had done for them. Jacob accepted the offer by promising to work for Laban for seven years if Laban would allow him to marry Rachel (because Jacob loved her). Laban agreed, and Jacob got to work so he could marry the love of his life. Jacob gets to work, and seven years flew by, and Jacob was ready to get married. Laban prepared the wedding feast and escorted Leah to the tent for Jacob that night instead of Rachel. The next morning when Jacob discovered that his uncle tricked him, he confronted him about it. Laban told Jacob that the customs (governing laws) did not allow the youngest daughter to get married before the eldest- so you know Jacob had to work another seven years. Laban gave Jacob Rachel to marry after the first week of his marriage to Leah- but he loved Rachel more.

Can you believe that Jacob's uncle deceived him with the promise that he would allow Jacob to marry Rachel? Laban had a hidden agenda, and he manipulated Jacob because of his love for Rachel. Laban realized that Jacob would work for a wage not standard, Jacob desired a wife, and Laban knew very well that the youngest would not be allowed to marry before the eldest in their country, and yet, Laban withheld that information from Jacob. Laban broke his promise by giving Jacob Leah, his eldest daughter, to marry instead of Rachel (the one he loved). Because Laban went back on his word, Jacob had to labour another seven years than was initially promised to marry Rachel. Though Laban cheated Jacob his promise through deceit, God sees things differently.

Did you guess the answer to my question? Yep, you got it- it's God. No one else can keep up with all those promises they make- and it's not because they don't want to. So what makes God so awesome that He remembers all His promises to keep them? God is sovereign; with the help of His word, I can think of a few reasons why:

- ➢ His ways are higher than ours. (see Isaiah 58:8-9)
- ➢ God's ways are past finding out. (see Romans 11:33)
- ➢ God cannot lie. (see Numbers 23:19; 2 Timothy 2:13)
- ➢ God cannot go back on His word- He says that if one of His words should return to him void (empty or unaccomplished), Heaven and earth will pass away. (see Isaiah 55:10-11; Matthew 24:35)
- ➢ He loves you with an everlasting love. (see Jeremiah 31:3)
- ➢ He honours His words above His name. (see Psalm 138:2)
- ➢ With God, all things are possible- they are not all possible with man. (See Jeremiah 32:17; 27).

God makes promises because He's all of the above and more. God is not like a man- God is, was, and will always be God all by Himself. God doesn't just make you big promises that He can't keep, because He feels good, or He intends to make a show- it's way more than that. God makes promises simply because He is faithful enough to keep every word. God makes promises because it is His expressed assurance to you that you can always depend on Him, and all your expectations met. God loves you, and He is willing to commit to you through the love He has for you. He re-inforces your trust in Him by being committed to what He said. Your needs and desires are no trouble to a sovereign God. You are precious in His sight, and for this, He will never neglect the fact that you are His (see Isaiah 43:4).

Many people make promises they know they'd never be able to fulfil: some are far-fetched, some they've forgotten about, and the rest were merely empty words. Just as Laban betrayed Jacob, we have all been let down and used. Jacob was honest and honoured his commitment to Laban; Jacob trusted him- but Laban was just a man. You can trust God's promises- He will never let you down. God will never go back on His word. He withholds nothing from those that walk upright. God will always keep His end of the bargain; He'll never deceive anyone.

Reflection

Think on these things…

> What promises have you made that you did not keep?

____

____

____

____

____

> It is safe to say that an un-kept promise is a deceit. Many times we commit to God, but we fail/ forget to stick to it. Will you ask God to forgive you by writing a brief word or prayer?

____

____

____

____

Your word is your bond, do your best to keep it.

GOD'S PROMISES ARE PRESENTED IN SEVERAL WAYS

God reveals His promise in several different ways, but until you learn to obey Him, He may not show them to you. God does not only choose to show His promises in the ways I have stated; however, it is out of obedience that you form a relationship with God that will cause you to live a life worthy of His promise. You may be able to relate to a few of these:

Divine Instruction

Judges 13:3-5, KJV

[3] And the angel of the Lord appeared unto the woman and said unto her, Behold now, thou art barren, and bearest not: but thou shalt conceive, and bear a son. [4] Now therefore beware, I pray thee, and drink not wine nor strong drink, and eat not any unclean thing: [5] For, lo, thou shalt conceive, and bear a son; and no razor shall come on his head: for the child shall be a Nazarite unto God from the womb: and he shall begin to deliver Israel out of the hand of the Philistines.

The children of Israel were disobedient, and God allowed the Philistines to take them into captivity, but God still had a promise to keep. God remembered the promise He made to Abraham, Isaac, and Jacob (Israel) to maintain their generation after them- even though the children of Israel slipped and forgot their promise to serve the Lord their God, Who, brought them out of Egypt, and through the wilderness. God planned to make sure that Israel remained under His care and His divine promise. While in bondage to the Philistines, God sent word through His Angel to Manoah's wife that she would have a son (though she was barren). "For, lo, thou shalt conceive, and bear a son; and no razor shall come on his head: for the child shall be a Nazarite unto God from the womb: and shall begin to deliver Israel out of the hand of the Philistines." (see Judges 13:5 KJV). For God to fulfil His promise, He had to have a chosen vessel to deliver a child. Because Manoah's wife was barren, that made it impossible for her to have a child. It had to be an act of God for her to become pregnant with a male child (see Luke 2:23). Sometimes things seem impossible, and God uses His Promises to bind us to Him to make man's impossible possible. Don't worry about what you can't do, but what God can do through you. Manoah's wife was given divine instruction not to eat anything that comes from the vine or strong drink, no razor would touch his head, and their child would be a Nazarite- consecrated onto God from the womb to the day of his death. He would be the one to deliver the children of Israel out of their enemy's hands. For you to receive what God has promised you, you must follow divine instruct by walking in obedience.

Do you see what one act of obedience can do?

A pre-requisite for receiving God's promise is obedience. They committed to honouring God in obedience to His divine instruction. When God sends us His word that He will bless us, He expects us to be obedient to receive it. After you've done the will of God, through your obedience, faith, love, and submission to God, then, you will receive the promise. I.e. When you're obedient to God, you will receive what He has promised you.

Judges chapter 13:3-5 says that God made two promises through His Angel. God made a promise that Manoah's wife would conceive and bear a child, though she was barren. The second promise was that the same child would be the one to deliver the children of Israel out of the hand of their enemies, the Philistines- here, God's promise brings surplus that not only benefited Manoah and His wife but the rest of the Israelites too. The only requirement was their obedience to God.

Your disobedience would keep you barren and unqualified to receive God's promises. Hence, the promise of God is not only for you but for others too. God wants you to be obedient by following His instructions. Manoah's wife was faithful in her obedience to God and delivered Israel from the bondage of their enemies. There is a plan intended when God makes you a promise, and you'll never know what that plan is until you obey Him. God's promise to you is a blessing that will be a blessing to others around you too.

Reflection

Think on these things…

➤ Has God sent you divine instruction?

____

____

____

____

➤ Are you obedient?

____

____

____

____

If God makes you a promise, expect that He will come through for you.

Now, let's look at another way in which God reveals His promises.

Divine Instruction With A Simple Command

Matthew 4:19 & Luke 5:1-4

Jesus presents a simple command to Peter and the men letting them know what would happen if they did what he said. Jesus uses direct circumstances as initial proof that He is faithful to His word when He challenged the faith of the fishermen. God defies all odds by making man a promise, and we do the same when we accept His promise. God is Sovereign, and He already knows what will and will not happen. Our minds cannot fathom all that God is capable of, so we have to wait and see. He will teach you how to, and He will help you to nurture it. The men already knew how to catch fish, but Jesus had to give them counsel on how to fish for men and nurture that promise by teaching others to do the same. "Follow me, and I will make you fishers of men" found in Matthew 4:19, KJV, is divine instruction with a simple command. It was a promised word to the men that would follow Jesus. What's remarkable about the text (see Mark 4:20) is that the men left what they were doing and followed Jesus' right away'. The men were already ordinary fishers, just like we are ordinary people, but following Jesus would make us extraordinary. Jesus wanted to make His point clear that if they followed Him, then He would make them (not just any ordinary fishermen) 'Fishers of Men.' That in itself is a unique title that later became a legacy. Jesus was telling them that He would teach them how to nurture their fishing skills to win humanity for God. In other words, following

Jesus gave the men hope that Jesus was a man of His word, and they could always count on Him because they received of Him.

Here, the word 'follow' signifies a command. If you don't come, you won't receive what God's about to give you. The fishermen acted upon Jesus' divine instruction and obtained their promise of becoming fishers of men (soul fetchers for God's Kingdom). To live a life of joy, goodness, peace, and fulfilment, you must do God's will. God's will is for you to obey Him, have faith in Him, love Him, and submit yourself to Him. Then, after you've done the will of God, you will receive the promise (see Hebrews 10:36). If Peter and the other men had not followed Jesus' instructions, they would not have received what He promised them. Luke 5:1-4 has a record of the divine guidance given to Peter. This passage of scripture demonstrates the willingness, humility, and accepting the act of obedience to follow.

Though the Bible does not state every detail of this event, one can only imagine the dialogue between Jesus and Peter. Let's look at a possible scenario from Luke 5:1-4:

> Jesus, seeing the boats on the sea and the fishermen washing their nets, said, "Launch out into the deep, set your net for a catch."

> Peter, challenging the accuracy of Jesus' command, replies "We've been doing that all night; what's different this time?"

> "Nevertheless, at thy word I will let down my net" was Peter's act of obedience.

Peter's obedience resulted in the men catching large amounts of fish that their nets broke and they had to beckon to their neighbours for help in carrying their catch to the shore. (see Luke 5:6)

In the current world crisis (COVID-19) instructions are being given to protect you in preventing the spread of the pandemic. You have to follow these instructions in taking the necessary precautions so you can remain whole and healthy. Many people fail because they refuse to follow basic instructions so they cannot reap the benefits of the promised word. You can choose to ride in obedience or die in disobedience. The songwriter rightly puts it: Trust and obey, for there is no other way to be happy in Jesus, but to trust and obey. How does one heed to divine instruction? The answer to that question is by doing the will of God. If you follow the instructions, you will reap the blessings of your obedience; but if you do not follow the instructions, you will not receive the promised.

Jesus wanted Peter to understand what the difference between leaning on his understanding is, from leaning on divine instruction. Peter received an overflow that he never would've gotten had he not been obedient. Peter's act of obedience brought him a surplus that he had to call for help. It proved that many of us have sleepless nights working tirelessly to reap from our strength and understanding, yet a simple command brought the increase. Though we toil, we will not catch any unless we follow divine instruction. The fishermen had to go back into the boat, launch out from the shore, let down their nets, and wait for the catch. Trust and obey means to remain while being obedient. It is out of obedience that you form a relationship with God, and from that same relationship, you will become fishers of humanity. God wants you to trust Him, and after we've done His will, you will receive what was promised (see Hebrews 10:36).

Following Jesus leaves a legacy that will be beneficial not only to you but to others around you. Your obedience to God, faith in Him, love for Him, and submission to Him will prompt you to follow Him. These fuels hope that Jesus is a man of His word, and you can always count on Him to deliver on His promises to you. All you have to do is follow Him.

Divine Instruction – You MUST Use What You Have

1 Kings 17:13-16, KJV

[13] And Elijah said unto her, Fear not; go and do as thou hast said: but make me thereof a little cake first, and bring it unto me, and after make for thee and for thy son. [14] For thus saith the Lord God of Israel, the barrel of meal shall not waste, neither shall the cruse of oil fail, until the day that the Lord sendeth rain upon the earth. [15] And she went and did according to the saying of Elijah: and she, and he, and her house, did eat many days. [16] And the barrel of meal wasted not, neither did the cruse of oil fail, according to the word of the Lord, which he spake by Elijah.

God told Elijah to go to Zarepath after spending some time by the brook called Cherith, where God had instructed ravens to feed him. There, Elijah met a widow who God told to sustain him. Elijah grew hungry, so he asked the widow to bake him a cake, and then she could prepare a meal for herself and her son. In the widow's estate, Elijah reassured her that the flour and oil she had would not go running out, but will be enough to sustain her household until God sent rain. Though the widow did not have enough for her family, she used what she had at Elijah's command. The widow was obedient to divine instruction that probably made no sense at the time, and made Elijah's cake first. Her act of obedience brought a surplus that she had enough left to sustain herself and her son until God sent the rain to the land (see 1 Kings 17:14).

For all this to happen, Elijah had to follow God's divine instruction to enter into that city, and the widow had to follow Elijah's instruction to use what she had to preserve their lives. Being a mother means she could've refused to do it because she wanted to feed her child. Being human means, the widow could've fed herself and her son, complained, and left Elijah for dead because he was a stranger. For the widow to receive that promise, she first had to follow divine instruction. Elijah was the widow's affirmation and hoped that God's word was the truth. Sometimes we would think that what we have is insignificant, but if we only knew what our little could do. Little is indeed much when God is in it. Use what you have so you may receive your promise.

When you are obedient, you receive what's on the other side of obedience because it goes both ways. Before God told Elijah to leave Cherith to go over to Zarepath, God said to him that He had instructed a widow there to sustain him, and that is what happened. Neither Elijah nor the widow received all the details, but they were obedient to God nonetheless. God covers you when you are compliant, so do not you forfeit your cover through disobedience. If God says "GO" you must be obedient. The person on the other side of obedience, has already received instructions to cover you. All you have to do is go. God provides the resources (in many instances) after you have obeyed Him. His provision is your cover. God is the One who covers you.

A young prophet named Elisha wanted a double portion of the anointing his master had. How did he obtain it? He followed divine instruction. While Elisha was under tutelage, he had to follow Elijah's guidance to receive his double portion, or else he would've missed it. Elijah knew that Elisha had asked for a hard (but not impossible) thing, yet Elijah only asked that Elisha do one thing. Elijah said, "...if thou see me when I am taken from thee, it shall be so unto thee, but if not, it shall not be so." (2 Kings 2:10, KJV). Elisha would remain focused so that he would not miss his promise. That may seem simple enough, but the journey from Gilgal, Beth-el, Jericho, and Jordan was not without distractions. Yet, Elisha obtained the double portion of anointing for which he had asked. When you are obedient, you will receive the promised. No matter how hard it may seem, remain focused, and you will receive your promise. Elisha may have had a little anointing for himself, though he was but a young Prophet under tutelage. He not only wanted to follow his master, Elijah, but he wanted double that anointing. (see 2 Kings 2:9)

Don't worry; God knows what He's doing. God knows the way because He is the way. It's the little things that leave the most significant impact.

The key here is to remain focused, follow divine instructions, and use what you have, and you will receive your promise.

Reflection

Testify…

➢ Has God come through for you in ways that you thought were impossible?

____

____

____

____

____

➢ What has God done for you with the little that you have?

____

____

____

____

____

It's the little things that leave the most significant impact. Allow God to bless your little so that you will receive your promise.

Divine Instruction – There's A Lesson To Learn

Jonah 1:1-4, KJV

[1] Now the word of the Lord came unto Jonah the son of Amittai, saying, [2] Arise, go to Nineveh, that great city, and cry against it; for their wickedness is come up before me. [3] But Jonah rose up to flee unto Tarshish from the presence of the Lord, and went down to Joppa; and he found a ship going to Tarshish: so he paid the fare thereof, and went down into it, to go with them unto Tarshish from the presence of the Lord. [4] But the Lord sent out a great wind into the sea, and there was a mighty tempest in the sea, so that the ship was like to be broken.

Often, the instruction you receive may not be what you want, or what you're willing to do, but your obedience is essential. Jonah thought to himself that the people of Nineveh did not know his God, they were enemies of Israel, they would not listen to him, and they would have perished either way. He may have thought that telling the people what God said would not have made a difference because they were so wicked. Remember, the promise of God is conditional, and in Jonah's case, the condition was for him to declare God's word to Nineveh. Jonah delayed the process when he boarded the boat to go to Tarshish, instead of Nineveh. He fell asleep on the ship (lost consciousness); The men on the ship threw Jonah overboard because he did not belong on the ship, let alone on that journey, and they thought he was the cause of their distress (high wind). A great fish swallowed him for three days and three nights so that he could reflect on what he had done (timeout for his disobedience).

When Jonah boarded the ship to Tarshish, he thought he could hide from God so he would not have to go to Nineveh. Little did he know that no one can hide from God and that his delayed obedience is disobedience. Nevertheless, he was not too deep in the fish's belly for God to make an escape route for him. While in the fish's belly, Jonah had to repent for not following God's divine instruction, and God heard his plea. God spoke to the fish, and it vomited out Jonah on dry land. (see Jonah 2:10). He was disobedient, but it added much value to the lives of the people of Nineveh because they repented as well.

Why is it essential for you to follow divine instructions?

If Jonah had followed God's divine instruction, he would not have gone on the traveller's boat with the cargo, and he would not have ended up in the fish's belly. Disobedience to God shows utter rebelliousness and lack of respect, and it can lead you into danger. It's as if you're telling God that He doesn't know best, and you will do whatever you want because you know better. "But the LORD sent out a great wind into the sea, and there was a mighty tempest in the sea so that the ship was like to be broken." (See Jonah 1:4, KJV). God did this to prove to Jonah that He was in control.

When you do not do what God says, it affects others. If they did not throw Jonah off the boat on the sea, maybe the other travellers would have been destroyed. If Jonah never went to Nineveh, all those people would not have repented. There are times when you may feel as if some people are incapable of change or repentance, and you may write them off. You must follow God's instruction. There are times when you'll allow pride to cloud your better judgment and make you blind to what God is doing in your life or the lives of others. But God is gracious, and He has mercy upon whom He will. It is not suitable for you to be angry at His decision to save the lost and use you to minister to them. God was still merciful to Jonah. It all worked out for good by God's purpose. The people repented, and Jonah learned a valuable lesson.

God is, but He punishes sin, so it's always best to do what He says.

Reflection

Think on these things…

➢ Have you been disobedient lately? If so, why?

____

____

____

____

➢ What lesson has your disobedience taught you?

____

____

____

____

The instruction is not always what you may want or agree with, but you have to be obedient to receive the promise, or in this case, learn the lesson.

Divine Instruction –
Wait On Your Promise

Luke 24:49, KJV And behold, I send a promise of my Father upon you: tarry ye in the city of Jerusalem, until ye be endue with power from on high.

Acts 1:4-5, KJV[4] And being assembled together with them, commanded them that they should not depart from Jerusalem, but wait for the promise of the Father, which, saith he, ye have heard of me. [5] For John truly baptized with water, but ye shall be baptized with the Holy Ghost not many days hence.

Jesus commanded the disciples that they should not leave Jerusalem but wait (tarry) there because their work would begin in that city, and He ascended so that they (His disciples) would receive the promise of His Heavenly Father. In His earlier days, Jesus told the disciples that more excellent works they would do than He did on earth (see John 14:12), and He knew they needed to wait for the empowerment of the Holy Ghost to be able to do it. They could've received the promise at His word, but God wanted them to wait so that they would receive such a sign because the task ahead was enormous. The disciples were promised baptism in the Holy Ghost, but they were unsure of what would happen or what that meant. It is possible that they were anxious, worried, or maybe afraid, but they just had to wait for the right time to begin the more excellent work on the foundation laid for them by Jesus. The disciples had to follow divine instruction- and that was for them to WAIT- it was just for the season.

The disciples had to wait for their anointing, but there is something else about the word 'wait' that makes it more interesting. When Jesus commanded the disciples to wait (tarry), they had to spend time in expectancy and time in agreement with each other. The waiting period built their character and faith in God. Their patience made them fully developed and mature- they lacked nothing when they received the Holy Ghost- as they gained the power to do everything that Jesus was able to do and more.

They knew they had to have empowerment from the Holy Spirit and that their entire life of ministry depended on it. If they weren't expecting anything, they wouldn't have been patient through prayer. If they were double-minded, they wouldn't have received their promise. It had not been many days, and yet the disciples were eager to receive the promise; the disciples were longing for that go-ahead; they needed the power to accompany the good news they carried, and so they had to wait. With the absence of power from on high, the sick would not heal, the lame would not walk, the blind would not see, the captives would not go free, sinners would not get saved, there'd be no growth in the body of Christ on earth, and man would not communicate with God.

You might be wondering what the significance of this story is, or how this even applies to your life. But I believe that God has called us to do more excellent works and all in His timing. Waiting on anyone or anything is never easy- especially if the wait time is longer than expected. Waiting can be one of the most annoying things to the most impatient person, and a bore for the person who doesn't mind waiting. But the essence of waiting is only discoverable in the process (what you do in the interim). Your willingness to trust, obey and wait, and desire to learn from all the hardships that come with waiting is of great importance.

If you believe with all your heart that God has called you to His promise (power from on high), and you're wondering- just as the people who heard the good news on the day of Pentecost- what you should do, or what happens next (see Acts 2:37). Then I implore you, as Peter did, to fully commit yourself to God, be obedient, have faith in God and submit yourselves to Him, and you will receive the promise (see Acts 2:38). Submit yourself to God, and you will receive the power you need to walk in the purpose God had intended for your life. God has already made you a promise that He has a grand plan for your life that will bring you into your real purpose. This promise is of benefit to you, your children, and for the next generation (see Acts 2:39)- and you can only accomplish those things through the power of the Holy Ghost. Plant yourself in prayer, separate yourself from the world for a season, and wait. When you shut the doors to the world, you open a window for the Heavenly dove to come down and breathe on you the comforting power He brings to do what you have to do.

Wait in prayer and fasting as the disciples did (see Acts 1:14). Whatever God has promised you, He wants you to wait in prayer and submission because prayer is the utterance of your faith in God.

Don't overthink the promise. Don't try to figure it all out on your own. Don't try to solve God's problem with your personal opinion or solution. God knows when you are unprepared or unready for the task, He has laid out for you to do, but you have to wait. God is greater, and He is the author and finisher of your faith. It may seem like it's too much to bear, and you're exhausted with fear, but you must wait on your promise. You might be bursting with enthusiasm to start the work, but you must tarry. You may see a need to share the Gospel the way Peter and the other disciples did because they knew that Jesus was the Christ Who had been sent to redeem man but WAIT!

It's not that the disciples were incapable of managing what the promise, but God did not want them to be anxious or move in their human strength. Instead, He wanted them to be patient and obedient so that His power would fully equip them for the signs and wonders that would follow them (see Mark 16:17-18). I can tell you that they were eager to do their Master's will- and who wouldn't be, after being named among the faithless generation when they could not cast the demon out of the young man? Not to mention the added pressure they faced waiting for Salvation's plan to fall into place. They have been waiting since they met Jesus. They had to wait for the crucifixion, burial, and resurrection from the dead. Then He asked them to wait (again) for the power. Their patience taught them discipline as they waited in prayer and fasting.

Acts 2:1-6 records the fulfilment of that promise to the men who would, after that, continue the more excellent work of Jesus Christ, on the day of Pentecost. The disciples were all in one place, expecting God's promise, in agreement with each other and with God. The anointing and power of God were like 'cloven tongues like that of fire upon their heads'. They were all filled with the Holy Ghost (they received the promise), and they all prophesied as the Holy Ghost gave them the power to do so.

Then they waited for the anointing that would later change them from ordinary disciples into Apostles who were empowered to deliver the good news to the world. Had they rushed the process, they would've prematurely forfeited their promise, prophesying vainly in ministry, and that would be utter disobedience. Just as the apostles were empowered for their purpose (as prophesied in Isaiah 61:1), you will be enabled for yours- you need only to wait.

Reflection

Think on these things…

> ➤ Do you trust God enough to wait?

____

____

____

____

____

____

____

The apostles received power for their purpose, and you will receive power for yours- you need only to wait.

Divine Instruction - God's Promise Is Greater Than Your Expectation

See Acts 3:1-11

A beggar laid at the gate called beautiful for many years. He was so accustomed to begging alms (gifts) that he got used to getting what he petitioned from the people as they entered gate beautiful to worship in the temple. This beggar had a disability and laid at the entrance of the temple every day so that those who passed by could hand him something that would've only sustained him for a short time. He may have never imagined that one day would appear that he would receive something that would maintain him for a lifetime. Peter and John were on their way to worship or fulfil their duty as stewards of the Gospel when they met the beggar who, of course, asked of them. Peter stood upright, filled with the anointing, and declared that "Silver and gold have I none, but such as I have give I thee: In the name of Jesus Christ of Nazareth rise up and walk." (see Acts 3:6, KJV). To everyone's surprise, the beggar got up rejoicing. Jumping, and frolicking about with glee. How happy he was that he had received such a gift. "Rise" was an instruction that shifted his habit of begging alms of temporary relief/ satisfaction to a life of thanksgiving to God that loosed the band of his infirmities. While his expectation was for him to receive alms, God's gift to him was more excellent. Healing of the sick, raising of the dead, restoring sight to the blind, and restoring strength to the lame- including this poor beggar- were all promised in the Gospel (see Isaiah 61:1).

God's promise is greater than your expectation, and in the beggar's case, he received healing for alms. The disabled beggar received a higher value than what he had expected. The beggar expected to earn some money, but God had another plan. It was a promised word with immediate effect all because the beggar already had high hopes of gaining something.

Let's observe this analogy:

> The beggar sought alms every day at the entrance gate to the temple where people go to pray and worship. The entrance to the temple was a beautiful gate, so it must've attracted a lot of people. Then again, Jews go into the temple (not Samaritans) for prayer and worship daily, and they are very generous- so one could say the beggar knew who to ask for alms. The presence of God is a beautiful place to be, and the beggar knew that this place would be a bonus. Go to that place and ask of God what you will because He knows how to bless you.

Divine Instruction (Command): "Look on us!"

> Beggar (You): Looking at Peter and John attentively while expecting something, did what was commanded of him (he already had faith he'd receive it)

> The Promised Word: "…such as I have, I give thee: In the name of Jesus Christ of Nazareth rise up and walk."

Can you imagine how the beggar felt when Peter told him they had no silver or gold to give to him? How disappointing?

Have you been praying for that money to cover the rent or groceries for the week, or even tried borrowing the money, but told to ask someone else? Maybe they don't have the money to give you, but they can give you a place to stay.

Such as I have is a better solution. Peter and John did not have what the beggar asked of them. However, they possessed an even more excellent gift to give to the beggar.

The lesson we should never forget is that 'Obedience is work'. Faith alone is futile. Verse 7 and 8 of Acts chapter 3 says that Peter took up the beggar and lifted him, and immediately his feet and ankle bones received strength. What a Mighty God we serve! In addition to both Peter and the beggar's faith was their work. The beggar could've refused to stand up. He could've refused anything outside of what he had asked for- but he didn't. He believed that he would've gotten something (anything- not just the money), and he got a more excellent gift.

Peter and John received power to do as prophesied in Isaiah 61:1, which Jesus read in the temple in Luke 4:18. It reads:

> Isaiah: "The Spirit of the Lord GOD is upon me because the LORD hath anointed me to preach good tidings unto the meek; he hath sent me to bind up the broken-hearted, to proclaim liberty to the captives, and the opening of the prison to them that are bound."

> Luke: "The Spirit of the Lord is upon me, because he hath anointed me to preach the gospel to the poor, he hath sent me to heal the broken-hearted, to preach deliverance to the captives, and recovering of sight to the blind, to set at liberty them that are bruised,"

The Spirit of the living God *[that raised Jesus Christ from the dead]* dwells richly in me; God has anointed me to spread the good news to all humanity: to the poor and needy, downtrodden, sick, wounded and oppressed. They shall know the God they serve is also their avenger. *[Emphasis added]*

Another interpretation of the scripture is 'Good News for the poor and oppressed', and the disabled beggar was poor and op-pressed; this is the greater work promised to the Apostles, and a promise that is greater than the beggar's expectation.

Acts chapter 2 shares the promise of the same Spirit that anointed Peter and John that brought good news and liberty for the dis-abled beggar in his time of need. That same Spirit has anointed me to remind you that your good news is on its way. Verse 25 of Acts chapter 3 says, "Ye are the children of the prophets, and of the covenant which God made with our fathers, saying unto Abraham, And in thy seed shall all the kindreds of the earth be blessed." I.e. God had already promised your forefathers that He would bless them and because you are heirs to such a promise He will bless you too.

There are times when you, just as the beggar did, ask God for a blessing. You may ask for some money to clear a debt, a little food for the week, a better life, or more time with our family- what-ever blessing you ask of God know that He always has something greater in store for you. Peter and John offered the beggar some-thing that would be more substantial to his life. God is a problem solver, and this beggar had had a disability since he was born. He was so accustomed to begging that he felt hopeless and could only afford a little to suffice him for a day, and probably thought he would only survive by begging. Can I tell you that God sees a greater need? You may look at our situation and convince yourself that you need to work harder to be able to afford the rent, but God wants to bless you with a house. What alms do you keep begging God? Do you find yourself at the same place every day still seeking and wanting more? What are you expecting of God? Let me tell you, God's promise is greater than your expectation! Your expectancy of God will bring you into a place of fulfilment. Your hope in God will lead you to the well of life. If the beggar expected alms and received good news, and the woman at the well expected only to quench her thirst with a little water from the well and received living water, how much more will God give you? (See John 4:13-14). God sees a greater need in your expectancy, which is why He made you a promise. If our earthly fathers know how to give us good gifts (being in their sinful nature), how much more will your Heavenly Father give- only if you'd ask of Him? (See Matthew. 7:11)

No one has to carry this once crippled beggar anymore to beg for alms. No one has to give him anything because he can now work for it. He is no longer a hopeless beggar. He no longer has to wear diapers, and no one has to clean him. No one has to bathe him or feed him.

Today is the day for you to start expecting more of God. Go before Him with expectancy in your heart because God is going to bless you. His promise to you has already set the grounds for expectation. It only starts with His command/promise, and your obedience and faith in God will take care of the rest.

Reflection

Think on these things…

➢ Has God exceeded your expectations?

____

____

____

____

____

➢ How did God do such a thing?

____

____

____

____

____

Indeed, God's promise is greater than your expectation.

Divine Instruction With Confirmation

Judges 6:12, 14 & 16, KJV; Also see Judges 6:36-40

[12] "... The Lord is with thee, thou mighty man of valour."

[14] "... Go in this thy might, and thou shalt save Israel from the hand of the Midianites: have not I sent thee?"

[16] "... Surely I will be with thee, and thou shalt smite the Midianites as one man."

Judges 7:9-15, KJV

[9] And it came to pass the same night, that the Lord said unto him, Arise, get thee down unto the host; for I have delivered it into thine hand. [10] But if thou fear to go down, go thou with Phurah thy servant down to the host: [11] And thou shalt hear what they say; and afterward shall thine hands be strengthened to go down unto the host. Then went he down with Phurah his servant unto the outside of the armed men that were in the host. [12] And the Midianites and the Amalekites and all the children of the east lay along in the valley like grasshoppers for multitude; and their camels were without number, as the sand by the sea side for multitude. [13] And when Gideon was come, behold, there was a man that told a dream unto his fellow, and said, Behold, I dreamed a dream, and, lo, a cake of barley bread tumbled into the host of Midian, and came unto a tent, and smote it that it fell, and

overturned it, that the tent lay along. [14] And his fellow answered and said, this is nothing else save the sword of Gideon the son of Joash, a man of Israel: for into his hand hath God delivered Midian, and all the host. [15] And it was so, when Gideon heard the telling of the dream, and the interpretation thereof, that he worshipped, and returned into the host of Israel, and said, arise; for the Lord hath delivered into your hand the host of Midian.

In your journey to unravelling your promise, God guides you by confirmation. Either by His Holy Spirit, His word, His people (witnesses), or circumstances. Gideon was one such man, who was guided by God through the confirmation of His word. Gideon was declared a 'mighty man of valour', and the angle commanded Gideon to go in his strength that he may deliver Israel out of the hand of the Midianites, but Gideon wanted a sign that he was hearing from God. God listened to Gideon's petition and gave him a sign.

Gideon did not think of himself as a significant man for many reasons. He stated plainly the reason why he could not be hearing from God (see Judges 6:15). Gideon said he was of least significance in his father's house, and his family is poor. Can you imagine telling God that you cannot do what He said because you didn't receive the proper training? What about telling God that you're not as knowledgeable as you think you should be? Just like Gideon did, you will have your excuses, but that doesn't stop God from confirming His promise to you, and it most certainly does not stop God from doing great things in your life.

Of a fact, Gideon and his family were the least in Israel, yet God declared him a mighty man of valour. He was a nobody, and anybody who's a nobody would want proof that they are more than that if somebody told them they were. As a human being, it is only natural that you act and speak the way you see things, but supernaturally, you are worth more than that. The innate sense is limited, but the supernatural sense is limitless. I.e. God sees more in you than you see in yourself, after all, He made you.

Like Gideon, there are times when you would think that asking for proof that you've been hearing from God means that you doubt Him and that you will stir His anger by it, but God will confirm He said what you heard. Nothing is wrong with wanting a sign to prove that you heard from God and that you do not imagine things. What you do with the confirmation is what matters. When you seek proof of God's promise, it is proof that you intend to do something about it. Looking at your natural abilities will cause you to doubt yourself many times. It's as if you're telling God, "No, Lord, what you're telling me is impossible. Do you think I'm strong enough for this?" Gideon had his excuses, but the Angel reassured him after each excuse that the Lord will be with him. Gideon already possessed what was needed, and God had sent him (see Judges 6:12, 14 & 16).

Judges 6:11 tells us that the Angel of the Lord found Gideon threshing wheat in the winepress. Gideon already knew how to use what he had; he just needed a little encouragement. He was convinced by confirmation (see Judges 6:33-40) to lead a vastly out-numbered Israelite army into victory over their enemies, the Midianite army, who had bullied them for many years. Gideon took courage when he overheard the Midianite soldier sharing his dream of their loss in the battle against the children of Israel (see Judges 7:9-15). Just like Gideon, you have the capabilities necessary to do great things; all you have to do is follow the divine instruction.

Your destination is not nearly as important as how you get to where you're going. Always seek God's confirmation (through fasting and prayers) and act according to God's divine instructions, to see if you're going in the right direction, and to ensure you're walking in His will and purpose for your life. If you acknowledge God in all your ways, He will show you what path to take (see Proverbs 3:5-6).

Judges 6:12, KJV, speaks of the premise on which you will receive confirmation. Your premise is and should always be: Surely, God has said it, and God has sent me. It helps you to discover your talents, your real shape, expose your strengths, find the right career or ministry, cause you to forsake pride, promote humility, and grow in wisdom, knowledge, and understanding. It gives you a testimony that God did what He said He'd do through you. Your premise defines your confirmation, and your confirmation positions you for more excellent works. You already have what it takes, do as what God says.

God allowed the Midianite Soldier to speak defeat over themselves as part of the confirmation that would encourage the Israelite army to defeat their enemy in battle. God's approval was not only encouraging, but it was empowering. The Israelite army was strengthened for victory as they won the fight against the Midianites.

Reflection

Think on things...

➢ What have you learned from your circumstances?

____

____

____

____

____

____

➢ Can you identify God's promise in your circumstances? If so, what are they?

____

____

____

____

____

> Have you ever asked God to confirm what He has said to you? How did He respond?

____

____

____

____

____

____

____

You already have what it takes, do what you God says.

Let's see what other ways we can identify God's Promises.

Letter From A Friend

I was at home one day when the Holy Spirit came directly to my ear and said these words

Dear Mighty Man/ Woman of Valour,

He that is faithful in a few things continue so in it- the Lord will multiply it in due season. Remember, ye are lacking in nothing, therefore, you MUST use what you have.

Signed,

A Mighty Woman of Valour.

God knows what you need, and when you need it. God spoke these words to me as a promise that He will provide the increase if I followed His instructions in using what I have. Now, I'm sharing these beautiful words with you. God can keep every word; watch and see.

God Lays The Promise On Your Heart

Luke 2:25-32, KJV

[25] And, behold, there was a man in Jerusalem, whose name was Simeon; and the same man was just and devout, waiting for the consolation of Israel; and the Holy Ghost was upon him. [26] And it was revealed to him by the Holy Ghost, that he should not see death, before he had seen the Lord's Christ. [27] And he came by the Spirit into the temple: and when the parents brought in the child Jesus, to do for him after the custom of the law, [28] Then took he him up in his arms, and blessed God, and said, [29] Lord, now lettest thou thy servant depart in peace, according to thy word: [30] For mine eyes have seen thy salvation, [31] Which thou hast prepared before the face of all people; [32] A light to lighten the Gentiles, and the glory of thy people Israel.

When you think about the heart, straightaway, you'd think about a flushing red organ beating inside your chest to circulate blood throughout your body. Besides pumping blood, the heart holds the key to your deepest desires, intentions, and emotions. But how does God lay a promise on this organ? The scripture says that Simeon was a just and devout man. The Hebrew translation indicates that Simeon was an upright and righteous man in the sight of the Lord. It also means that Simeon was submissive, seeking diligently of the Lord and did what was right in his heart and his deeds. The scripture may not have given much detail, but the words and devout says a lot about Simeon. His relationship with the Lord was one that carried much reverence and value. He was aware of the presence of the Lord and what God was saying to him. His heart was already open to the Lord, as he was earnestly seeking God (waiting for the consolation of Israel) when the Holy Ghost made it known that the promised child is present. How amazing is that?

This scenario brings us back to what a promise is. God's promise to us is an everlasting covenant that allows Him to bind Himself to man. God honours His word and reinforces our trust in Him by being committed to what He said- so, He makes things happen. It was prophesied years ago that a Messiah would come. God promised Simeon that he would not die until he sees the fulfilment of this promise. God honoured His word to him. He anticipated the move of God. His devotion meant that he was open to hearing from God, and because of this, the Holy Ghost led him into the temple to see the Messiah. Mary and Joseph took baby Jesus to the temple to present their offering of purification and present the baby to God, as it was the law. Simeon took hold of the baby boy (Jesus) and blessed him then he asked that the Lord would allow him to die in peace because the Lord had been faithful in His promise to him. The Bible does not give all the details as to when God laid the promise on Simeon's heart. It did say he would not see death until- that means he lived his days with high expectation, longing, and hoping for the coming Messiah. A just and devout man such as Simeon knows that God would continue to be faithful- even to the rest of His people. Simeon testified that he had seen the promised child, he had seen the future the child would bring to the world, and how the Lord has prepared redemption through his Son so that the world as a whole shall see it- including the non-Jews.

You must understand the promise and when it is laid on your heart. When something is laid on your heart, it is not so easy to get rid of it. You'll have an urge to see it come to pass; you'll search for it every day and everywhere-, and that's how Simeon felt. The descendants of Israel had long awaited this promise- but this one man, as the Bible mentions him- was devout (he was a just man) and had also lived through the dreary absence of God's hand in their land. Simeon had been waiting for a while to see the promised Messiah that would take away the sins of the world, and reconcile humanity with the true and living God.

The way I see it, no matter how long it takes, God will do as He had promised. Whatever God has laid on your heart, don't think for a minute that He has forgotten you. God cannot change, and God cannot lie. His words must accomplish what He said they would. Simeon did not die until he saw the promised child, but he saw him because God revealed it to him before he died- and so will you. You will never leave this earth until you see what God has promised you. Then, your life will be a testament to the faithfulness of God. Your life will be proof that God never lies. David said that he would have fainted unless he had seen the goodness of the Lord in the land of the living (see Psalm 27:13). That means that God came through for him in a time when he needed to see it most- when he was almost at the point of giving up. God will come through for you.

Reflection

Think on these things…

➤ What promise has God laid on your heart?

____

____

____

____

➤ Has God delivered His promise?

____

____

____

____

Be assured that God will not allow you to see death until you have received all He has promised you.

Guard Your Promise

Nehemiah 4:17-18, KJV

[17] They which builded on the wall, and they that bare burdens, with those that laded, everyone with one of his hands wrought in the work, and with the other hand held a weapon. [18] For the builders, everyone had his sword girded by his side, and so builded. And he that sounded the trumpet was by me.

Nehemiah heard the news that the city Jerusalem that it was in a desolate state and that the people had been taken captive by the Babylonians. God had placed a great deal of care on Nehemiah's heart and made the provision, through King Artaxerxes, for him to go back to Jerusalem to help the people rebuild the walls and the city. God wanted His people and the city to return to its former glory, and Nehemiah was determined to rebuild the wall, but that came with its fair share of troubles. When God makes you a promise, He first lays it on your heart. Your responsibility after that is to guard that promise with all your heart. Do not be deterred by the naysayers, gainsayers, idle jesters, and jokers. Rest assured, God is doing a work in you too, and you cannot come down.

You cannot fulfil a promise without faith- it is impossible without it. You cannot have blessed assurance in something that you have not built up, and that is your expectation that God is not slack on His promises, neither will He go back on His word. Practice daily portions of faith in the word of God and the promises He made you. God will surely keep His promise to those who remain faithful to Him. When the fiery darts of doubt seem to prevail, you must guard your promise with all your heart because your life depends on it. Pray and stand on the promises of God. When you live solely by the word of God, it means you are guarding your promise. If you are not living by God's word, it means you are not safeguarding your promise. Nehemiah and the people of Jerusalem defended the promise God had made to them with the sword they held and the work they put in to rebuild the city and its walls. You have to guard your promise with the sword of the spirit. I.e. the word of God.

Be encouraged in the many times He has come through for you and others, so your faith won't fail. Guard your promise, according to Ephesians 6:10-18. You MUST take courage in God's strength. You MUST depend wholly on the force, might, and power of God. Be bold, ready and always alert in your stance against opposition to God's promise in your life. Stand flat-footed against the rulers of darkness in this world: the ones who cause affliction through hard labour, and strange diseases, the evil you cannot see with your naked eyes, sacrifices to the devil, the practice of witchcraft, killing the poor, and every contrary way to the will of God—always praying for direction so that you will not forfeit your promise.

The troubles and doubt will not last; only the promises of God will prevail. Whatever God has promised you, guard it with all your heart. Nehemiah 6:15 records the completion of the wall at Jerusalem- all because the people had a mind to work. Nehemiah and the people of Jerusalem guarded the promise by working together. "For thus saith the Lord, that after seventy years be accomplished at Babylon I will visit you, and perform my good word toward you, in causing you to return to this place." (see Jeremiah 29:10, KJV). God made a promise that the exiles would return to Jerusalem, and they did because the people guarded the promise.

Be not deterred, be determined, and guard your promise.

Reflection

Think on these things…

➢ Have you lost sight of your promise lately? If so, why?

____

____

____

____

____

➢ How will you guard the promise God made to you?

____

____

____

____

____

Be not deterred, be determined, and guard your promise.

Your Promise Is Revealed In A Vision

Genesis 37:5, 7 & 9, KJV

Chapter 37 of Genesis tells the story of a young boy named Joseph, who found favour in the sight of God and man. Joseph was among eleven brothers (all of the same father). Jacob loved Joseph more than all his other brothers because he had gotten him at an old age. Jacob loved Joseph so much that he made him a beautiful coat, one that had many colours, but this stirred the jealousy and hatred of Joseph's brothers against him. Joseph's brothers despised him to the point where they could not speak kind words to him. But as time went by, Joseph began to have dreams that neither of them could understand. When he shared the first dream with his brothers, they mocked him.

Here is the dream:

5 And Joseph dreamed a dream, and he told it his brethren: and they hated him yet the more. 7 For, behold, we were binding sheaves in the field, and, lo, my sheaf arose, and also stood upright; and, behold, your sheaves stood round about, and made obeisance to my sheaf.

Their scorn grew when Joseph shared his second dream with them. His father scolded him too, yet he wondered what the dream meant.

Here is the second dream:

[9] Behold, I have dreamed a dream more; and, behold, the sun and the moon and the eleven stars made obeisance to me.

One day, Jacob sent Joseph to check on his brothers while they were tending to their father's flock. Joseph left home in search of his brothers, and when he met them, he had only been with them for a little while when they tore his beautiful coat, that his father had given to him as a gift, and threw him into a nearby cistern that was empty. They were planning to kill Joseph because they thought he was boasting and mocking them that his dreams meant that they would bow to him. They may have only thought about getting rid of Joseph, but their father suffered in grief for many years.

Likewise, you may have suffered because of other people who were jealous and felt intimidated by the dream that God has shown you. You may not fully understand the meaning of your dreams, but believe it nonetheless. It may seem impossible because of where you are right now but believe in the vision that God has shown to you. You may be accused of lying but believe in your dream. Even if they threaten to kill you, believe in your dream. Your opposition means that you've found favour with God and He's getting ready to bless you.

When people don't understand what God has promised you, they may mock you or think to do evil against you.

Reflection

Think on these things…

➢ What dream has God revealed to you?

____

____

____

____

➢ Do you believe it will come through?

____

____

____

____

Genesis chapter 37 ends with Joseph being sold off to the Egyptians- to an officer named Potiphar, who was also the captain of the palace guard. But God used this situation to bless Joseph. For you to achieve the promise, you must leave your comfort zone. When God gives you a vision, He will give you provision

God's Promise Is Better Than Your Comfort Zone

Fear, superstition, doubt, loss of control, and abandonment are all the negative emotions associated with coming out of one's comfort zone. But can I tell you that it's okay? It's quite natural to feel this way when their haven is under threat of being compromised by the unknown or the unfamiliar. Have you ever heard of anyone who'd be willing to leave their comfy pillow top mattress, with the fluffiest cushions and cotton-soft linen that is to die for, to sleep on the cold hard floor? Think about the significant differences between a warm bed that almost folds around your body, giving you enough comfort and support that makes you so relaxed, and that floor that is so hard you'd think your limbs are going to break off the minute you sit on it. You can make your mental comparisons, but I know I'd stick to the bed that I know. Joseph's life was that pillow top mattress, and just the thought of going down to Egypt as a slave- among a people that didn't serve his God- would make anyone quiver. God had some nerve. God knows that you'll never make it in your comfort zone, all laid back and unbothered. He has to force you out of your will through discomfort, simply because His promises are better than your comfort zone. Joseph's life was too perfect, being the favourite son and all, God had to get him out of the clouds, put him on land to serve the nation of Israel in a time they'd need it most. Joseph trusted in God.

Sometimes we misunderstand God's promise, and as such, you can misinterpret what God says.

While in Egypt, Joseph was promoted three times. He was given charge over the livestock and the house of Potiphar - except his wife of course. He was then promoted while he was in prison, and Pharaoh promoted him. When God promotes His people, it may seem to them that the circumstances are unfavourable and undeserved, but all things, good and bad, work for good because God loves us. God will take you from your little town or circle of five and establish and favour you among the diplomats of the world. All you have to do is follow His lead, believe in the dream God revealed to you, and remain humble. I've never heard of slaves being happy, or imprisonment being a life one would covet, but God blessed Joseph in such a way that he found favour with man wherever he went. Joseph became Ruler over Egypt. How could this be? A Hebrew, second in command to Pharaoh - King of Egypt? That's absurd!

Paul rightly puts it, "O the depth of the riches both of the wisdom and knowledge of God! How unsearchable are his judgments, and his ways past finding out!" (See Romans 11:33, KJV). No one can honestly say that they've understood from the get-go where God was leading them until they started to notice the changes in and around them. Luke 5:39, KJV, says, "No man also having drunk old wine straightway desireth new: for he saith, the old is better", and yet, we anticipate living our best lives forgetting that God's ways are higher than ours. No man has ever desired to move from a place that he's comfortable with to go to a place where he's a stranger. We keep forgetting that time and time again; God has proven that His promise is unfamiliar and unconventional in every way.

God is more than capable of using your circumstance to fulfil His promise to you. He is wiser than you and I, of course, He's knows best. When you let go of what you know for what God says, then you'll understand that not everything that seems hostile is out to harm you. Stepping out of your comfort zone is a risk you might not want to take, but it is worth it.

Reflection

Think on these things…

➢ What blessings have you received through unfamiliar/ unfavourable circumstances?

____

____

____

____

____

➢ How did you recognize God's hand at work in your life?

____

____

____

____

____

When you let go of what you know for what God says, then you'll understand that not everything that seems hostile is out to harm you. God's promise is better than your comfort zone.

Shanique Davis

There's A Process Attached To Every Promise

Genesis 45:5-11, KJV

There is a process attached to every promise, and Joseph had to go through it. He was sold into Egypt by his brothers. His master's wife seduced him. They imprisoned him. They forgot about him in prison. Then he was summoned to a higher calling- a promotion that only God Almighty could've given him- all based on the promise God had revealed to him. He served in Egypt as second to Pharaoh, who was the king. God revealed His purpose for Joseph when there was a great famine in the land. God preserved Israel's bloodline through Joseph's discomfort when his brothers came to Egypt to buy food during the famine. He reassured his brothers that he was not angry with them and that he knows that it was all the will of God, and it all worked out for good. He said,

5 Now therefore be not grieved, nor angry with yourselves, that ye sold me hither: for God did send me before you to preserve life. 6 For these two years hath the famine been in the land: and yet there are five years, in the which there shall neither be earing nor harvest. 7 And God sent me before you to preserve you a posterity in the earth, and to save your lives by a great deliverance. 8 So now it was not you that sent me hither, but God: and he hath made me a father to Pharaoh, and Lord of all his house, and a ruler throughout all the land of Egypt. 9 Haste ye, and go up to my father, and say unto him, thus saith thy son Joseph, God hath made me Lord of all Egypt: come down unto me, tarry not: 10 And thou

shalt dwell in the land of Goshen, and thou shalt be near unto me, thou, and thy children, and thy children's children, and thy flocks, and thy herds, and all that thou hast: [11] And there will I nourish thee; for yet there are five years of famine; lest thou, and thy household, and all that thou hast, come to poverty.

Stepping out of your comfort zone is a new feat that will cause you to act and think differently. There are times when you'll face what seems like the harshest situations and bear the pressures that you've never imagined- BUT GOD. Your comfort zone is too restricted; when you begin to loosen the reigns on your life that you've held on to over the years, God will step in so that He can have total control to do great wonders for you. If you choose to remain in your comfort zone, you'll run the risk of being disobedient to God, living a stagnant, unfruitful, uninfluential, and unproductive life. Admit it, if you're comfortable with where you are, that means you don't need to think about what you're doing or how you're living. Everything will be one flat, mundane, autopilot situation that will eventually get tiring and boring. There is a calling and purpose for your life, and believe it or not, you have a divine assignment attached to you. God will push you out of that comfort zone so He can fulfil His purpose in you. Your discomfort is never without purpose; you have to trust God through it. The thrust that God gives you will propel you into your divine purpose. Feeling overwhelmed in spiritual warfare is one that I can attest to, but God has been my help. God has not and will never leave you to walk alone. You may have to pray more, fast more, seek Him in a higher study of His Word, but He's there with you. The discomfort you'll feel is not unto death. It's not to destroy you either; it may be quiet there, but God's voice is enough to guide you, and His presence is enough to light your path.

From your comfort zone, the Lord will harness all the potential that you've had buried all your life. His grace will give you the courage to unearth the untapped power you have to advance in His Kingdom. His call will force you to turn to and depend entirely on Him, more than anything or anyone else. For God to do something different in your life, He has to separate you from your place of familiarity. God wants to take you places. I'm sure Joseph has never even dreamed of going to Egypt. I mean, why would he, when he's so comfortable living in his father's house- having everything to his heart's content? God wants to make you known; God wants to enlarge your territory of influence; God wants to make you more like Him- in such a way that people will glorify Him. He wants to cut you loose from your reigns. God wants to bless you and make you a blessing to others. If He doesn't remove you from your comfort zone, you'll never experience the heights and depths of His love for you, and what you can do through Him. Learn to walk in humility before God and man and learn how to wait on God. You may be in a situation that you believe makes absolutely no sense at all. Your process may seem and feel like a waste of time. You may be asking God, why is this happening to me? But it's all His plan to fulfil His purpose in you.

Don't be afraid to leave your place of familiarity for strange lands- don't even think for a moment that God will take you out into the wild and let you go. God knows how you feel, and He knows that the water you'll cross with Him is deep; He knows the journey is lonely, but He ALWAYS promises to be there. The Lord was with him, so Joseph was prosperous, even while he served in the Egyptian house. Wherever God's love takes you, He will cause you to prosper. God chose some of the most unfavourable circumstances to bless Joseph to fulfil His promise.

Joseph's brethren bowed themselves to him in honour of not returning the evil they had done to him. The children of Israel became a great nation, and they prospered in Egypt as the Lord had promised. (See Genesis 50:17-21)

Joseph has been through his fair share of betrayal and disappointment, the promise that came to him in a vision had to fulfil.

Reflection

Think on these things…

➢ What disappointment/ betrayal have you suffered, so see your dream fulfilled?

____

____

____

____

____

____

➢ How did God turn your situation around for good?

____

____

____

____

____

____

➤ Joseph forgave his brethren because they were only doing the will of God. Will you forgive your brethren who have betrayed you?

____

____

____

____

____

____

____

➤ There's a process attached to every promise.

PERFECT OBEDIENCE

Hebrews 5:8-9, KJV

8 Though he were a Son, yet learned he obedience by the things which he suffered; 9 And being made perfect, he became the author of eternal salvation unto all them that obey him;

The New Testament of the Holy Bible records samples of perfect obedience portrayed in the life of Jesus. While on earth, Jesus was said to be fully God and fully Man. The fact that He was entirely God meant that He could not do wrong because of His supernatural character. Also, being fully man would suggest that Jesus was capable of doing wrong through the weakness of the flesh. However, it is remarkable how he held up the banner of righteousness in the earth through His perfect obedience. The records say that Jesus had been born of a virgin (Mary, his mother). He was tempted in all points as we are, and yet, without sin; suffered much rejection, shame, persecution, and having done the will of His Heavenly Father on earth, gave His life as a ransom for humanity to go free. His experience and testament are a legacy that laid the foundation for Christianity today. In other words, Christ's sacrifice during His mortality brought humanity immortality through much faith and active obedience to the divine instruction from His Heavenly Father.

Before Jesus took on the sins of the world so that humanity could have a chance at eternal life, He was mocked, scorned, tempted, rejected, beaten, put to death by a ruling of the courts, and public opinion. All this was part of God's divine will and plan of Salvation for our lives. All humanity had been missing the mark set by the law that handed down to Moses, a servant of God, and so, humanity could not afford to pay the penalty for their sin. Jesus was God's way of dropping all charges against us, and He became the ultimate way of escape from eternal death and damnation. Obedience is and always has been the condition on which God makes promises to man. God has made known this ruling since His first command to Adam in Genesis 2:17, KJV, "But of the tree of the knowledge of good and evil thou shalt not eat of it: for in the day that thou eatest thereof thou shalt surely die." By now, it is safe to say that all disobedience to God's divine instruction is sin. Sin because man has missed the mark God has set for them to follow. It is the same for all deviation to the law God laid out for a man that death is inevitable, but Jesus' perfect and active obedience to the cross is our peace in God and an escape from His wrath. How amazing is that?

The world would die in sin and shame- had it not be for Jesus' perfect obedience. If the Son of God had to be obedient, why do you think you are above it? Who will go and save Adam's fallen race? Jesus offered Himself for our ransom. His act of obedience meant that He had to do whatever it took to see the plan of Salvation through to the end. Humanity rejected Him, His people, the peculiar nation whom God called to serve Him, the same people who looked for a Messiah did not even think Jesus was worthy to be called the Messiah. He was mocked and scorned- all through this- He obeyed God. What if God had taken the cup when Jesus prayed that night in the garden? What if He had chosen His omniscience and left you and I to the curse of death? Jesus could've resisted the law and His arrest, but He didn't. He could've defended His innocence, but He didn't. Obedience led Jesus to the cross to die for our sins. It was obedience that caused Jesus to press on through persecution. It was obedience that taught Him to stay in constant prayer to His Heavenly Father when He wanted to give up, and it was obedience that cried for mercy while He was hanging on the cross.

In the earlier years of Jesus' life, He taught the people regarding the importance of obedience. Found in Matthew 22:37-39 are the two most important laws/ commands of God. If a man obeys these, then they are in right standing with God and are worthy of receiving their promise. When you choose to love your neighbour as yourself, you will see no need to be rebellious or disobedient but submissive in honouring them. When you love God with all your heart, soul, and mind, you will learn to submit in obedience to Him. Remember, the will of God is for you to love and honour Him by loving your neighbour. Once you've done the will of God in the earth, you will receive the promise. Your level of humility will determine your level of obedience. Jesus humbled Himself unto His death- even on the cross. To obey it isn't always easy, but it is worth it.

Let's face it. We live in obedience to the laws of the land (see Hebrews 13:17); children obey their parents in the home (see Ephesians 6:1); we comply with the rules governing our workplaces, and we live in submissive to our spouses (see Colossians 3:18). We live in obedience to God out of duty, our love for God (see John 14:15), and love for each other (see Matthew 22:39). If Adam and Eve understood the importance of obedience, we would've never had the nature to do good and evil. We must contend (daily) for the right and abstain from disobedience-which is to sin against God and ourselves. Sinfulness will cause you to miss the mark, and when you miss the mark, you miss your promise. When you miss your promise, you'll lose your blessing. God gave you free will, how do you plan to make the most of it? Will you continue to be disobedient so that grace (sacrifice) may abound? Disobedience leads to sinfulness, and sinfulness never pleases God.

Today, the cross not only represents the love God has for us, but it is a symbol of the active obedience of Jesus Christ to the divine will of His Heavenly Father on earth- an exemplary life that we ought to follow. Jesus shed His blood for you and me because of His love and obedience. It was one man's disobedience that plunged us all into guilt, shame, debt, and death, and it is one man's obedience that delivered us from guilt, shame, and death. As Ezekiel Azonwu rightly puts it: "We have all worked in sin and death was minimum wage, but if it wasn't for Christ, we would've almost got paid."

Reflection

Think on these things…

> Looking back at your life, can you recall when you decided to disobey God because humanity didn't like what you God called you to do?

____

____

____

____

____

> Is there any memory of turning back from the mantle you God gave you to carry? If so, why?

____

____

____

____

____

➢ What steps will you take toward active obedience?

____

____

____

____

____

____

There'll be times when you'll have to give up your rights for the sake of your obedience and submission to God, but do not be disheartened, God will always honour your obedience.

YOU CANNOT HELP GOD WITH WHAT HE PROMISED YOU

Genesis 16:1-4, KJV

[1] Now Sarai Abram's wife bare him no children: and she had a handmaid, an Egyptian, whose name was Hagar. [2] And Sarai said unto Abram, behold now, the LORD hath restrained me from bearing: I pray thee, go in unto my maid; it may be that I may obtain children by her. And Abram hearkened to the voice of Sarai. [3] And Sarai Abram's wife took Hagar her maid the Egyptian, after Abram had dwelt ten years in the land of Canaan, and gave her to her husband Abram to be his wife. [4] And he went in unto Hagar, and she conceived: and when she saw that she had conceived, her mistress was despised in her eyes.

Here's a *possible* dialogue that would help us to analyse the scripture a bit:

Sarai: Hmm, Since I have no children, and the Lord seems to have forgotten me, I'll do it myself. Why God has refused to bless me with a child of my own, I'll have to make it happen. I may not be able to have a child, but I have a servant who'd do it for me if I ask her.

Also, Sarai: Abram, my darling, go in onto my servant so we can have a child. Maybe this is the only way I'll ever be able to have one; perhaps this is what the Lord meant when He promised me a child- it's been ten years and still nothing.

Abram: As you wish.

Convinced the plan would work- Abram took heed to his wife's concern and went into her servant- Hagar.

In the scripture provided, you can see where Sarai, Abram's wife, became despondent- to the point where she convinced Abram of a scheme she devised for him to have children.

Have you ever felt as if you were too mature or too old to do something? Sarai must've felt worthless, disappointed, distressed. Just like Sarai, many of us are discouraged when we are promised something and can't see it coming. Frustration sinks in, and you see how happy everyone else is with what they've achieved, and all you can do is imagine it. Sarai was anxious- even though she laughed at the promise (see Genesis 17:16-17).

Sarai may have asked herself: But, why was it taking so long? God, where are you? Have You forgotten Your promise to me? Is it Your will to put me to shame?

Her biological clock was ticking, and the longer she waited on God, the older she grew. Time was running out; it seems, and it was becoming impossible by the minute. All the reasons why any woman would take that leap. Can you understand Sarai's di-lemma? She was nothing short of emotional and desperate. That's why she gave her servant to her husband. She probably thought her servant was younger and more capable of giving birth. God had made her the promise too long ago for it to be still possible-maybe He forgot.

When you try to help God, you end up making a mess of what should've been the perfect plan. If you can remember correctly, this was the same woman who laughed at the promise of her conceiving- all because she thought she passed the age to do so. Blinded by her doubt, she felt she could make it happen- having dwelt with her husband in Canaan for ten years (this was ten full years after God had promised them a child).

Abram also doubted his human capability when God promised them a child, and so, he and his wife thought they could help God with the promise. The only way you can help God is by being obedient to Him; God couldn't care less about what man can and cannot do. When you use your age, bodily functioning, timeline, and all things natural to determine the outcome of all things supernatural, you'll regret it. It's not your readiness that moves God but your willingness to fulfil God's promises despite the faults you find in your natural abilities. Stop listening to the biological clock that ticks from faith to anxiety. God wants will-ingness by faith.

Abram and his wife had no other choice but to believe what God had promised them. Abram, being convinced of God's prom-ises, and despite his age and wife passed the age of giving birth, he would become the father of many nations. God's promises will always defy man's logic. Sarai hasted in bringing forth her premature concept of God's promise by allowing Abram to lay with her maid, Hagar, so that she could bring forth Ishmael. Mischief is the fruit of our interference with God's promise, and Sarai almost forfeited her promise through her misconduct. God may not have revealed every detail of His promise to her, so she thought she had to be the one to make it happen. She misunderstood her authority, and that's not what God said. Even though God gave Abram a measure of faith, he doubted and laughed at God because he considered his age and state. When God fulfilled His promise, Abram's name changed to Abraham (Father of many nations), and Sarai's, name changed to Sarah (Mother of nations).

Sometimes we make decisions that God didn't consent to, and when our will births trouble, our hearts are not at peace with it. We would later realise that God had nothing to do with what we convinced ourselves, and all we had to do was wait.

We are not people with a hopeless end, but an endless hope. God's promise will always outweigh the man's opinion. God's sovereignty will not allow room for us to help Him- other than our display of obedience.

Who could've told Sarai that all God's promises are yea and amen? Which is all the more reason why God would come through on His promise to them. He gets the glory, and His glory doesn't lie in man's ability- if He doesn't show up, then He's a liar- and He's not a man that He would lie. It was accounted to Abraham for righteousness because he still managed to utilise the measure of faith God gave to him. Where is your faith in God? Wait on God; don't let the doubt you have in yourself stand in the way of your blessing because you cannot help God with what He promised you.

Reflection

Think on these things…

➤ What are some of the promises that God made you that seemed too far-fetched?

____

____

____

____

➤ What have you tried on your own, instead of depending on God?

____

____

____

____

We are not people with a hopeless end, but an endless hope. God's promise will always outweigh the man's opinion. God's sovereignty will not allow room for us to help Him- other than our display of obedience.

GOD'S SURE PROMISE

Genesis Chapters 22

What if God made you a promise, then gave it to you, and then tested you with it? Maybe you'd say that's not the God you serve; He'd never do such a despicable thing. Well, He's not wicked, but He tests us to make sure we're ready for what He has in store. Previously, we analysed Sarai and Abram's desperation and their willingness to help God with the promise He had made to them. At the time, it seemed quite impossible because they were both old and passed the age where they could have any children, but God did just as He had promised them and gave them a son. They called him Isaac, and they loved him very much.

In Genesis chapter 22, precisely ten chapters later, God told Abraham to go offer up his promised child (Isaac) as a burnt offering (v 2). This wouldn't have made any sense to some of us today, because it's not something we'd want to do. Besides, who wants to give up their only son or only child after waiting to have that child for so long? That didn't seem like much of a blessing. God swore by the promise He made back in Genesis chapter 12 (v 2-3) that He would bless Abraham and multiply his seed, so why would God want Abraham to sacrifice his only son? I wonder if God is a murderer? But we'll never understand the command of

God until we're obedient to the instructions we're given. A promise is always there for us, but until we're compliant, we'll never obtain it. God has a way of testing us with what or who we love the most to see (prove) what or who we love the most (see Psalm 26:1-2). When you give up a person or thing of importance, God will not withhold any good thing from you (see Psalm 84:11). Isaac did not die, but God was impressed by the love Abraham displayed for Him.

God wanted Abraham to know the God he served. So, every time God makes a promise, He reveals another character trait He possesses. On the mount, when God provided the ram for Abraham to sacrifice (instead of Isaac), God revealed Himself as Jehovah-Jireh, which means The LORD will provide or See (v 14). When we obey God, He withholds nothing from us (v 16-18). The promise of God is conditional as it is a test, and Abraham passed that test. Verses 3-15 of Genesis chapter 22 tells a remarkable story of the love Abraham had for God.

Here is the story:

> *God instructed Abraham to go to Moriah to sacrifice his only son that God had promised him (whom he loved). Abraham saddled his donkey with his chopped wood and took with him his son and two of his servants. Abraham couldn't risk having his servants witness him, sacrificing Isaac, so he asked them to stay at a distance so he and his son could go and worship. Like every other sacrifice Isaac may have witnessed, he noticed that they only had the chopped would and the fire- but no sacrifice. Abraham responded to Isaac's curiosity by saying, "My son, God will provide himself a lamb for a burnt offering..." They got to Moriah and Abraham arranged the wood*

for the sacrifice, tied Isaac, and laid him on the arranged wood. With heart-pounding heavily, tingling feet, sweating profusely as the moisture leaves his mouth through his pores, Abraham picks up the knife, Oh wait, that's just me.

I don't know if he was nervous, but I know I'd be.

So Abraham picks up the knife, and as he was about to do the unthinkable,

Isaac trembling in silence,

The Angelic audience at the edge of their seats [gasp in astonishment] …

God calls to Abraham from Heaven, "Abraham, Abraham! Lay not thine hand upon the lad, neither do thou anything unto him: for now, I know that thou fearest God, seeing thou hast not withheld thy son, thine only son from me."

Phew, that was close. I know it may be hard to believe that this happened, but it did. God reaffirmed Abraham of the benefit of being obedient with an oath,

"By myself have I sworn *[as He could swear by no one else]*, for because thou hast done this thing, and hast not withheld thy son, thine only son: That in blessing I will bless thee, and in multiplying I will multiply thy seed as the stars of the heaven, and as the sand which is upon the seashore; and thy seed shall possess the gate of his enemies; And in thy seed shall all the nations of the earth be blessed; because thou hast obeyed my voice." (See Genesis 22:16-18) *[Emphasis added]*

God sealed His promise to Abraham with an oath, a guarantee that it cannot be changed, and Abraham received that oath ten chapters later.

Ten chapters might be a day's read but in all that time (days, weeks, months and years) God was preparing Abraham to receive his eternal blessing- he and all that would come after him. Abram was not yet at the place to gain his favour, so it took him many days, weeks, months and years to get it right. Though he was old, he was also very young in the faith, and that made him unprepared for his eternal blessing. God had to allow Abram to build his confidence in Him so that He could seal the promise.

You determine how long your ten chapters last as your destiny depends on your obedience. Hebrews 6:13-19 describes God's sure promises. They are convinced because He seals it with an oath and He cannot lie. Because of this very fact, we, who have received such promise, should not doubt that God will come through for us. Even so, it is safe to say that God has our backs. After the oath God made to Abraham when He swore by Himself, there was nothing left for Abraham to do because he had already proven his love and loyalty to God. God did not need Abraham; God only needed his obedience. Once the obedience to God's divine instruction is complete- so, He makes things happen. When God's fulfils His promise in your life, it brings Him glory. Hold on to your promise, remain steadfast and obedient to God- and after you do His will, He'll seal it with an everlasting oath.

Reflection

Think on these things…

➢ Is there anything or anyone in this world that you love more than you love God?

____

____

____

____

➢ What or who will you give up for God?

____

____

____

____

You should never love anything or person more than you love God. If God chooses to test you with what He obas blessed you with, do not be afraid to offer it back to Him. Believe that the same God Who blessed you before will give you double times over what you sacrifice for Him. You can never tell who will be blessed by your obedience in offering up your sacrifice of love to God.

GOD WILL DO AS HE PROMISED

Exodus 14:19-22 & 27-28, KJV

[19] And the angel of God, which went before the camp of Israel, removed and went behind them; and the pillar of the cloud went from before their face, and stood behind them: [20] And it came between the camp of the Egyptians and the camp of Israel; and it was a cloud and darkness to them, but it gave light by night to these: so that the one came not near the other all the night. [21] And Moses stretched out his hand over the sea; and the Lord caused the sea to go back by a strong east wind all that night, and made the sea dry land, and the waters were divided. [22] And the children of Israel went into the midst of the sea upon the dry ground: and the waters were a wall unto them on their right hand, and on their left.

[27] And Moses stretched forth his hand over the sea, and the sea returned to his strength when the morning appeared; and the Egyptians fled against it; and the Lord overthrew the Egyptians in the midst of the sea. [28] And the waters returned, and covered the chariots, and the horsemen, and all the host of Pharaoh that

came into the sea after them; there remained not so much as one of them.

The Exodus represents the departure of the children of Israel from Egypt to the Promised Land. The bible records their journey across the Red Sea as one of the most miraculous events in the history of humanity. God separated the Israelites from their enemy who oppressed them for many years (see Genesis 15:13).

When God promised the Israelites a land flowing with milk and honey, He gave it to them. God made the same promise to their forefathers, and He was faithful in delivering that promise, but they had to go through a process; the wilderness was that process.

God separated the Israelites from the things that sapped their lives through harsh labour. The brickwork and the work the field was hard (see Exodus 1:13-14). Sometimes living a life of promise is hard, as it was never easy for the Israelites. Even though they managed to cross the Red Sea, it was still hard. Not long after the Israelites had crossed the Red Sea and headed into the wilderness, they had sudden remorse for leaving what they were used to behind. They wandered in the desert and contended with many enemies before they would inherit the promised land. They started comparing the wilderness to Egypt and the food they were accustomed to there, so they murmured against Moses and God; in other words, they murmured against their promise. The journey through the wilderness was a state of disfavour, emptiness, and discomfort. The land was uninhabitable, and it was a reminder that they needed to get to the place that God had promised them- the land flowing with milk and honey.

Today, the wilderness represents a state of lack and impoverishment that beams distress in such a way that it causes people to complain about where they are, rather than where they were going. God took the first step by redeeming Israel from slavery, but their finite minds could not conceive the beauty of their freedom.

Nonetheless, the Exodus brought newness and holy change to the lives of the Israelites. They now had access to the promises of God. Their crossover not only meant the Israelites changed from rags of slavery to priesthood, but it also meant a change to their physical and spiritual diet. They had to renew their covenant between themselves and God, set structures in place with leaders to perform their Godly duty so they could enter the Promised Land as God's people.

God wants you to go and grow through your wilderness for you to inherit your promise. Be patient as your promise is straight ahead of you. You may not be able to control the hopelessness or frustration you feel, but there's a lesson in it. There will even be times when you will not see a way out, but keep believing in the promises God made you. God has been faithful in the promise He has made you. The same God Who brought the Israelites out of Egypt, through the wilderness, into the promised land will deliver your promise too.

You are promised a clear path out of all your troubles (see Psalm 34:19). You are guaranteed daily bread (see Matthew 6:11). God promised to strengthen you when you're weary (see Psalm 40:29). God promised His presence when you feel as if you're alone (see Isaiah 41:10). When you go through the roughest days of your life, God promises to be there for you (see Isaiah 43:2). Best of all, when you feel lost or stranded, God has promised you a place of bountifulness (see Exodus 3:17). When God makes you a promise, you must be patient in your faith that His promises are sure and secure (see 2 Corinthians 1:20).

His word says He is just God, and he cannot lie. His promise to you means more to Him than His name, and His Word can never return to Him unfulfilled. What's impressive is that if your earthly parents know how to give good gifts, what about your Heavenly Father, the God Who is in control, and rules and reigns over Heaven and Earth, wouldn't He give you better gifts? (See Matthew 7:11) There's no obstacle of doubt or delay that can stop God from staying true to the promise He made you.

Here is your Father's promise to you:

- ➢ Your children, the work of your hand, your crops and livestock will be blessed;
- ➢ Your basket of storage will never run dry (God will send help, and you will remain blessed);
- ➢ Everywhere you go you will be blessed;
- ➢ The Lord will fight against them that fight against you; He will even cause your enemies to be at peace with you (see Deuteronomy 28:3-14)

Simply put, everything about you will be blessed!

God said He would make His people fruitful, multiply, and then bring them into a land they could call their own. The nation would be prosperous, and most importantly, they could rest. Your promise is your blessing from God, and it is still available.

God will surely do as He promised you, be patient.

Reflection

Testimony and Thanksgiving…

➢ What promise has God made you?

____

____

____

____

____

____

➢ The Israelites crossed the Red Sea with a song of praise. What praise will you sing to God?

____

____

____

____

____

____

➤ Will you write to God a Prayer of Thanksgiving?

____

____

____

____

____

____

God kept His word to the Israelites when He gave them a safe journey through the Red Sea and kept them from their enemies (see Exodus 14:27-28). Isn't it fair that you trust Him to do what He said He would do?

HOW ARE GOD'S PROMISES FULFILLED IN YOUR LIFE?

Now that we've gotten through the many ways God's reveals His promises to us, we can put into context the three (3) main ways in which God fulfils His promises in our lives.

You will realize that they are co-related, and when applied to your life, the results will be amazing. By now, you should know that obedience to God's divine instructions is the key component in unlocking the promises God made to you. The other components: willingness to surrender and faith & love, are the binding agents that will cause your life to be more fruitful and fulfilling.

Obedience to Divine Instruction

Genesis 2:16-17, KJV

The first-ever command that God gave to man says this,

[16] Of every tree of the garden thou mayest freely eat: [17] But of the tree of the knowledge of good and evil, thou shalt not eat of it: for in the day that thou eatest thereof thou shalt surely die.

Man failed to obey God's command and has since given birth to death. Many other stories are recorded so you and I can learn and understand the importance of being obedient to God. Obedience is our submission to God's authority through faith in Him. It is an essential part of our life, and we cannot obtain any good thing without it. God has no other motive but to bless us, and once we're obedient then He has no other choice to do as He has promised. Obedience will always be better than sacrifice because obedience is an act of worship. If you love God, you'll do as He says. Your submission to God will attract the blessings He has promised you. The more you obey God, the more like Him you'll become: holy, loving, just, merciful, and kind. Obedience to God is His will for your life, and if you're not doing the will of God, you won't receive the promise. Your compliance not only opens the window for a blessing, but it also shows God that you truly love Him, you'll be loyal to Him, you'll trust Him, and you know Him.

Here are some results of obedience:

> Noah and his family were saved during the Great Flood
> (see Genesis 8:18-19, KJV)

[18] And Noah went forth, and his sons, and his wife, and his sons' wives with him: [19] Every beast, every creeping thing, and every fowl, and whatsoever creepeth upon the earth, after their kinds, went forth out of the ark.

We all have a fair chance at Salvation because Jesus was obedient to death (see Philippians 2:8, KJV)

[8] And being found in fashion as a man, he humbled himself and became obedient unto death, even the death of the cross.

When we sin against God, it means that we have missed the mark. If we are all working diligently to meet the higher calling through Jesus Christ, we must follow the divine instructions we're given. Disobedience leads to sin, and a clear example of this is King Saul. Saul's disobedience prevented him from remaining as King of Israel. Saul was already appointed King over Israel, had he waited for his anointing he would have kept his reign. God instructed Saul to kill the Amalekites and all that they had. Instead of following God's instructions, Saul took it upon himself to save the best (what he liked) of what they had to sacrifice to God. Saul's impatience caused him to disobey God, and he was ripped from his role as king over Israel (see 1 Samuel 15:28).

God wants to bless you through your obedience, so don't miss your promise by dragging your feet. There is a saying that goes: The will of God is best understood in retrospect. I.e., you may never understand what God is doing now but looking back (after all He has done for you), you will appreciate it. Go, even when you don't understand. God requires your obedience- that is how He makes things happen. When you're obedient, you're blessed, but you gain wisdom from God's knowledge and foresight to prosper in all your endeavours. Go and do what God says!

Willingness to Surrender Your Will for His

Psalm 23, KJV

[1] The Lord is my Shepherd; I shall not want. [2] He maketh me to lie down in green pastures: he leadeth me beside the still waters. [3] He restoreth my soul: he leadeth me in the paths of righteousness for his name's sake. [4] Yea, though I walk through the valley of the shadow of death, I will fear no evil: for thou art with me; thy rod and thy staff they comfort me. [5] Thou preparest a table before me in the presence of mine enemies: thou anointest my head with oil; my cup runneth over. [6] Surely goodness and mercy shall follow me all the days of my life: and I will dwell in the house of the Lord forever.

In addition to being obedient to God's diving instruction, you must be willing to surrender your will for His. You must be willing to surrender your will over your life to receive God's promise.

Let's take a closer look at Psalm 23. David expressed the total control he allowed God to have in his life when he boldly declared, "The LORD is my Shepherd." When the Lord is your Shepherd, you will lack nothing! The Shepherd will lead you into green pastures to feed and give you rest, the living fountain of water to quench the thirsting of your soul; He'll supply your every need, and you will be satisfied. The Shepherd will lead you on a glorious path as He has promised. Though you face the dreaded crisis- Christ still is. You'll not need to fear because the Shepherd is always near. You will be blessed openly by the provision of your Shepherd, even when your enemies are present. Your favour will overflow from head to toe- you'll have more than enough. Yes, undoubtedly, unquestionably, your fellow mates, goodness and mercy, will go with you on your journey, and you will have a home in the presence of your Shepherd now and forever.

When you recognized and understand that you will never make it on your own (without God), you will have no choice but to surrender to God. David's life is a testament that his flesh was prone to many weaknesses (pride, greed, murder, and adultery), and God's will for him was far more significant and far better than his own will. David knew that he could neither keep himself from danger nor sustain his breath- he had to completely surrender his will, body, and heart so that he could indeed live for God. If you have the desire to serve God, there must be self-denial (see Matthew 16:24).

A shepherd's job is to lead the sheep to find food and water, rest and comfort, shelter, and protection wherever they go. You are the sheep of God's pasture, and the voice you listen to is your Heavenly Shepherd. No sheep should have the capability to move about without the Shepherd because the He has an obligation to His sheep. God is the good Shepherd because He gives His life for the sheep (you and I). When you and I were as sheep going astray (doing our own thing and having our way), we surrendered to (return) to God, who is the Bishop of our souls (see 1 Peter 2:25).

Willingness to surrender everything to God means you want what God wants, you desire what God desires for you, and you'll go wherever He leads. The next time you repeat the twenty-third Psalm, listen carefully to the words you speak. Surrendering to

God is the message preached from Genesis to Revelation, and it doesn't get better than that. You will never become the person God wants you to be as long as you're holding on to your will, and you'll never receive what God has promised you. God wants you to do His will on earth, and you do His will when you surrender to Him. God cannot have His way as long as you have yours. You save yourself a lot of stress when you surrender your life to God. Isn't God Lord of your life? Why won't you surrender to Him? How often have you sung these hymns: 'I Surrender All,' 'I've wandered far away from God, Lord, I'm coming home,' and 'He wants His way in thee'? If you fully surrender your will for God's, then He will be your all in all.

Give God the privilege of taking care of you the way that He has promised, so that nothing else will matter after you make your last breath. You need God even more than you think. You can trust God- no need for doubts. You may never understand God's perfect purpose and intent for your life until you surrender to Him. When you surrender fully to God, life begins at its best. Acknowledge God's sovereignty in all situations. In all your ways acknowledge Him, and He will direct your path (see Proverbs 3:5-6). You must release your conversation, character, and conduct into God's hands- no strings attached. Raise that white flag as high as you can because God has a better plan.

A willingness to surrender your will for God's is the best thing you will ever do for yourself. When you surrender your time, talents, and all, it only means you're getting out of your way. Disobedience only prevailed because of the free will that man keeps abusing- not that free will is all bad- but it had brought us into a place of lack and disarray. We have the potential to destroy ourselves when we get to decide all the way (see 2 Timothy 3:2-4).

The scripture says that it is in God that we truly live, breathe, and have our being, i.e., we aren't truly living our best lives without God or His guidance. It is never easy to surrender your desire, intention, and worship, but it is possible. When you are living honestly and openly before God, you will allow Him total and free access to breathe on you and change you- making you more like Him each day. Lose the hold you have on your life, release your will for God's, and let Him guide you into the place He has promised.

[24] … If any man will come after me, let him deny himself (see Matthew 16:24, KJV). If you desire to obtain your promise from God, you must be willing to surrender your will for His.

Faith & Love

Your faith in God and love for Him will cause you to walk in obedience to his instruction, and it is your obedience in Him that highlights your life as being fully surrendered to Him. Obedience and surrendering fully to God is also worthwhile through your faith and love for Him.

Matthew 22:36-40, KJV

36 Master, which is the great commandment in the law? 37 Jesus said unto him, Thou shalt love the Lord thy God with all thy heart, and with all thy soul, and with all thy mind. 38 This is the first and great commandment. 39 And the second is like unto it, Thou shalt love thy neighbour as thyself. 40 On these two commandments hang all the law and the prophets.

The love that you have for God will cause you to do a lot of things that other people would say is crazy, it looks stupid, they'll turn up their noses, mock you for doing it, but God will be pleased. Do all things must to His glory and His honour. God has not given you the spirit of fear. Instead, He has given you His Excellent Spirit that empowers you, perfects His love in you, and gives you a sound mind. In your journey to obtaining your promise, you'll find that the love of God is rich and pure, and it'll enable you to do great and mighty things. The love of God is not about good feelings, and it's not as casual as some would treat it. The love of God makes Him perfect and sovereign- it's an undeniable reality. Any discussion about love has to commence with God; it's who God is. The word of God says that His love for you is everlasting. Unlike many of His promises, His love is unconditional because while we were His enemies, He sent Jesus to die for our sins.

God's love is our guide (see Psalm 119:105). God's love is for our benefit and His glory. Loving God with all that is within you; to love God is to love what His heart beats for, and that's His people. Your love for God will make you take a stand for what is right- man's moral standards will not always justify it because God's standards are higher- but God will be pleased, and glorified. Love equips you to trust God (see Proverbs 3:5-6).

Abraham's love for God convinced him for the promises God made to him. Daniel kept praying because he knew in whom he believed. Esther chose to perish if she had to as she went to see the king save her people. It was God's love that added favour to Gideon when he was named a mighty man of valour. Job loved God too much to turn away, so he acknowledged that it is the Lord who gives and takes away. The three Hebrew boys refused to bow before idols or worship other gods because they already knew the true God. David defeated Goliath by the faith he had in God. Joshua commanded the sun stand still because he had faith in God. These faithful men and women loved God so much that He had no other choice but to come to their rescue- no one denies what and who they love. Their love for God was higher than the culture that challenged their faith in Him.

It takes faith to show love, and love wins every time. It is measureless and long endures the tests of time- supplied by an all-sufficient God, it is just what you need to live your best life. When you love God, you live by His commandments.

All things work together for your good because you love God, and He called you to His promise. For faith to be complete, you must act in love. You need faith and love to work according to the divine instruction you're given. Without faith and love, you cannot please God because it is impossible to please Him without it (see John 14:15). God wants you to have confidence in Him even when you don't understand.

The love you have for God forms a correlation with faith that positions you for the fulfilment of His promises in your life. Your love for God and trust in Him put Him on the spot to do what He said He would. It shows Him off and draws believers to Him. Your love for God will always set Him up to fulfil His goodwill and purpose for your life- imagine that.

Faith and love work together (see 1 Corinthians 13:13). If you do not believe that God will come through for you, you will bow to your circumstance. You may not know where you're headed, but God knows the way. Even if it's strange to you, it doesn't mean that it's unfamiliar to God. In paths you do not see, He promises to guide you. The word of God is a lamp unto your feet and a light unto your path.

You might be wondering why you have to go through what you go through if God loves you, but all things work together for your good. God chose you because He loves you. God calls you beloved because He loves you. God promises to make a roadway in the wilderness to lead you, and rivers in the desert. God's love will sustain you through your dry times, gloomy days, and sleepless nights- even when you feel He's far away. God's love makes you, His friend.

God doesn't require any of His people to have great faith- though some do more than others- He requires that mustard seed amount of faith, combined with our love- so, He makes things happen. When you love God, you are not only blessed, but you gain exclusive access to His promises.

Loving the God that genuinely and undeniably loves you pays off. You'll be blessed so that you can be a blessing to others. Your second and third generations will be blessed- a thousand generations will be blessed. When you become saturated in God's love your life will testify to the Lord, and the world will know who you are and Who's you are; and on that final day of judgement, when God receives His heir, you will have confidence because you represented the love He called you to display.

Faith and love (charity) go hand in hand (see 1 Corinthians 13:13). You have a responsibility to sign God's Heavenly contract by faith; His words are sanctioned and sanctified by His Spirit. Let your faith activate your promise and watch God work. Your confidence will enlarge your capacity to let God's blessings flow throughout your life.

Reflection

Think on these things…

➤ Do you genuinely love God and have faith in Him? If so, say why.

____

____

____

____

____

____

➤ Why does your obedience matter to God?

____

____

____

____

____

____

➤ Have you fully surrendered your will for God's will?

____

____

____

____

____

____

____

God makes things happen when you do His will, and His will is for you to obey Him, love Him, have faith in Him, and fully surrender to Him.

DON'T LOOK BACK

Genesis Chapter 19

Lot had separated himself from Abram, as Lot thought the plain (Sodom) was a good place to live, so he settled there because it looked good. Who wouldn't want to inhabit a land that was lush and well-watered everywhere- even as it was the garden of the Lord (see Genesis 13)? Lot had chosen for himself all the plains of Jordan; he dwelled in the cities of the plain and pitched his tent toward Sodom. Verse 13 continues- But *[little did he know]* the men of Sodom were wicked *[evil, morally wrong, playfully mischievous]* and sinners *[who are reprobates]* before the LORD exceedingly *[to a great extent]* *[emphasis added]*. The beauty deeply enthralled Lot before him that he chose to settle before Sodom- before the people that would later be destroyed by God- and this was the beginning of Lot's demise.

The story in Genesis 19 talks about a man named Lot, who lived with a wife and two daughters in the city called Sodom and Gomorrah. One night, two angels came by his house to warn him of the destruction to come upon the city because the sins of the people there displeased God, and He was about to destroy that city. God was merciful to Lot and his family (see Genesis 18:16-19), and God wanted to save those who were not in opposition to righteousness. The scripture says the angel took Lot's hand, and his family with him, and led them out of the city before God destroyed that city. Lot and his family were warned not to look back because they too would perish.

God was taking Lot's family from where they had been compromising their faith by turning a blind eye to the wickedness they saw, and He wants to do the same thing for you. Whenever God is taking you somewhere, He expects that you will trust His doing. God has already promised that He will care for you because you are His, and He must fulfil every word He has promised you. If you have to look back at what you have to leave behind, it means your heart's desire isn't what God desires for you, but your heart's desire is what you're leaving behind. If God tells you not to look back, of course, He has better in store for you.

When you look back, you will lust at what you have to leave behind. When you look back, you will become unthankful. When you look back, you will lose confidence in God because you do not trust Him enough to do what He said. Do not look at your possessions the way Lot's wife did. She did not just look back as if she had dropped something, Lot's wife gazed with regret at all that they had to leave behind. She had already started to miss where she was coming from and had no clue how to trust where God was leading them. So, she looked back. I can only imagine having to leave all that I had worked so hard to achieve. Maybe I wouldn't want to leave either. Maybe Lot's wife was the President of a Women's Club in Sodom. Perhaps she was the envy of the city because of all that she possessed. Maybe, just maybe, she was happy with her life the way it was. How could she start over when she already had it all? Lot may not have seemed to care about leaving what he had behind, but his wife did. She lingered behind

Lot and their two daughters. Caught in her dilemma, and just like that, she looked back, and she became a pillar of salt.

Lovest thou Me more that these- what will your answer be? The question God is asking in the words of this song is: Do you love these (things) more than you love Me? What is it that you're holding on to that you think is more significant than God's promise to you? Isn't God your all in all? Think about the peace you'll forfeit; think about the needless pain you'll have to bear. It's not because you're not praying, it's because your priorities aren't on the right things.

I know you're used to taking care of yourself, but how much heartache has that caused you since you attempted? Let God do it for you because He knows what to do. Don't worry about the money, the clothes, gifts, and trinkets- look to the place that God has prepared for thee nourished with all that you'll need. God doesn't care about your popularity; He cares about your prosperity (in Him).

I've always heard the saying, "We cannot leave what's sure for the unsure", which means, we can't let go of what we know for the thing we don't know. I've already seen what earthly things can do. Why should I let go of all that I possess for 'a promise'? What if it doesn't come work out? I've never seen God, so how do I trust that He'll do what He said? I think God is just asking for too much.

Your indecision will not delay time. Not having a made-up mind will not change what God is about to do. Looking back only leaves you with regret. You'll start imagining the good that could've come of what you had and where you've been, but the more you start looking ahead at what God is doing in your life is, the more you'll appreciate your loss. God knows best. I'm not telling anyone to leave their bread for a grain of rice, but if God says it then go, and don't look back. If God took you out of a bad situation, don't look back.

The children of Israel looked back at what they had in Egypt and began to murmur; their bodies fell in large numbers in the wilderness; neither did they see nor enter into the promised land. Cut yourself loose from the past that seems to hold you back from starting your journey to your promise. Go where God sends you, and don't look back because that's not where you're going. You have a decision to make; if you're in the same dilemma as Lot's wife was- perish the thought.

Reflection

Let's hear your testimony…

➢ What do you fear leaving behind for God's promise? Why?

____

____

____

____

➢ What have you had to leave because your whole life was at stake?

____

____

____

____

If you look back, it means that you've said "No" to what God has promised you. Have faith in God and what He promised you would come through.

DON'T LOSE CONFIDENCE IN THE PROMISE GOD MADE YOU

Numbers Chapter 13

God commanded Moses to gather a ruler from each tribe of the children of Israel to send as spies into Canaan (the land He promised them). The men went to prove the land that God had promised them to inherit. They would determine whether the people were weak or resilient, few or many, whether the land was fertile or not, and if the cities are secure, and they were to return to camp with samples of the fruit of the land. After 40 days, the spies came back to Moses and all the congregation of the children of Israel.

Thus said their report,

"We came unto the land whither thou sentest us, and surely *[what God had promised is not a lie]* it floweth with milk and honey, and this is the fruit *[confirmation]* of it. Nevertheless *[But even so, anyway, regardless]*, the people be strong that dwell in the land, and the cities are walled, and very great; moreover, we saw the children of Anak there…" (see Numbers 13:27-28, KJV) *[Emphasis added]*

The spies returned to camp with good and bad news. Let's examine a *possible* dialogue among the spies after their trip to Canaan.

Spies: We're back from Canaan, where you sent us to examine the land. Indeed, the land has everything that the Lord has promised us. It is fruitful! Look at these (grapes, pomegranate, and twigs).

But, there is one other thing, the people who are living there are much bigger than we are, the cities are great and secured by walls. Besides, Giants live there.

Giants are living down South; Giants are living in the mountains, and more Giants are living by the sea- near the coast of Jordan." *[How will we ever be able to possess the land?] [Emphasis added]*

Caleb pleads: "Hush. Be Quiet, people. Let us arm ourselves and take the land from the Giants now because we are more than able to conquer them."

Other Spies: "We can't stand up against these Giants because they are too strong for us."

*The people murmured, spoke against the promise, their doubt surpassed all that God had done for them in the wilderness

Spies: "The land we saw is full of huge people, and we're no match for them. They're descendants of Anak! If we go into battle, they'll defeat us. We're nothing but grasshoppers before them, and that's how they see us too."

They reported to Moses and the rest of the people that the land was fruitful as they revealed the cluster of grapes, pomegranate, and twigs they brought back. But the land had been occupied by strong people, their cities were enormous- and guess what? They are GIANTS. The spies did confirm that there were giants in the land.

Is this a joke? Giants? What Giants? Who said anything about Giants?

The children of Anak were descendants of the Nephilim family- a family of very tall people (see Genesis 6:4). The children of Israel seemed like grasshoppers in Canaan when compared to the Giants in the land of promise.

Sometimes you'll receive bad news that would cause you to think that the promise God made you is no longer valid, but do not lose your confidence in God. Your greatest victories can come from what seems like defeat, but God has a way of turning everything around- supernaturally!

Will you believe the report of the Lord or the report of man?

Believe the report of the Lord. The children of Israel had to contend with Giants, people who were naturally bigger than they were, to inhabit the promise. They could've walked away from the promise, but they didn't, and neither should you. Remain hopeful in God's promises, fight the good fight, and endure hardship as a good soldier. Even when the promise you receive is not what you expected, don't turn up your nose and murmur. Erase the negative perspective (what you think God is saying or doing) and listen to what God says. Do not allow what you see or hear to discourage you. God could've given the land to the Israelites just like that, but He knew that Israel had a bigger problem, and that was faith in Him for the promise. God wanted to bless them, but they would never receive the promise without faith. It looks silly to be fighting for a piece of land somewhere when God could wave His hand and grant Israel the land of the giants, but it was not without purpose. Some of the Israelites must've thought it'd only be a waste of time to fight these huge people, but in all of that, two men stood up- Caleb and Joshua- and encouraged the people that God was with them if only they'd trust Him.

DON'T GIVE UP, WAIT ON YOUR PROMISE

When God makes you a promise, you must remain steadfast. Be unmovable. Be faithful. Be persistent and be dedicated to your faith in God. God cannot lie because it is not in His nature to lie. For you to possess the promised, you must NEVER lose your confidence in God. Take heart, as Joshua and Caleb did, and believe what God says and watch God lead you to your promise. When you have confidence in God, it puts Him in the spotlight to prove Himself and prove that what He has promised you will be done. Your faith in God is your agreement that you will wait for Him to come through for you in His timing. Do not allow the creditors to rush you. Do not let the loan officer stir up doubt in you. Do not allow the enemy of your soul to plunge you into disbelief. God has said it, so, He will do it. I've had days when I wanted to doubt God because of all that was happening around me. I was unemployed, limited on funds, out of groceries for over a month, and I kept hearing God whisper to me that all things work together for good and that I should wait for Him. He never left me, so I know He will never leave you to face your storms and hurdles alone. He will face your giants for you.

Just remember that amid every crisis, Christ (still) is. There are too many reasons why you should never lose confidence in God. He is a keeper, and He will keep you. He is all-sufficient, and He will sustain you for every season. He is the same yesterday, today, and forever. Though the seasons change, God NEVER changes. He moves differently- but He's still the same God. His move in each season is relevant. God moves as your Healer (Jehovah Rapha) in your season of sickness. In your season of need, God moves as your Provider (Jehovah-Jireh). He is a Healer and Provider, yet the same God. God is ever-present and ever relevant. God promised to be your Provider, Healer, Protector and Defence, Light and Guide, Banner over you, and He will be all of that and remain the same God. All-sufficient and All-Powerful God is He that has called you to obtain His promises.

Whether your obstacle or enemy is a spiritual or physical giant, do not be afraid to overthrow it with your faith in God. Whatever God has promised you already belongs to you. Whatever God has promised you, already has your name on it. By faith, Joshua and Caleb entered into the promised land- neither of the other spies did because they lost their confidence in God. Do not lose your confidence in the promise God made to you.

What's happening in your life is happening for you, not to you. You do not have to become whatever you go through. God gave you measure of faith to navigate under challenging times, so do not give up on God. Encourage yourself in the Lord, and let patience have her perfect work in you. Do not you're your confidence in God, because if you do, you'll miss out on what He has promised you.

Reflection

Let's hear your testimony…

➢ Have you lost your confidence in God? If so, why?

____

____

____

____

➢ How badly do you want what God has promised you?

____

____

____

____

God never changes. God never lies, and He never misleads anyone. He knows the way because He is the way (see John 14:6), so don't lose confidence in God.

THROUGH IT ALL

2 Timothy 1:12, KJV

For the which cause I also suffer these things: nevertheless I am not ashamed: for I know whom I have believed, and am persuaded that he is able to keep that which I have committed unto him against that day.

God tested Adam and Eve in the garden before they disobeyed Him by eating the forbidden fruit. God tested Abraham when He told him to leave his father's house to go into a land of promise, and then offer his son (who was also promised by God) as a sacrifice. King Saul threatened David's life after he defeated Goliath, so David went hiding in a cave. Elijah fled to save his life after Jezebel had threatened to kill him. God promised the children of Israel an inheritance of a land flowing with milk and honey. These people were all proven by tests because God wanted to ensure their hearts were at the right place to receive His blessings. God also wanted to show that His character would be in them through the tests He allowed them to go through.

Throughout the Bible, the word test signifies 'proof by trial.' Hence, God proves His sovereignty when we remain steadfast and unmovable in our faith that His promises are true. Either you trust and obey Him, or proclaim Him a liar through your insolence and disobedience. According to James, the testing of our faith develops perseverance and faithfulness in our walk with God. He is the ultimate source of help and where God guides He always provides. The test not only proves you are worthy through your obedience, but it shows God is worthy of your trust. No test makes sense until it's time for a recap. A trial proves your knowledge and skill, and it determines who you are and who you can be. The Apostle, Paul, was tested, and from his test, he understood what it meant to be full, high, abased, and satisfied. Paul knew that he could do all things (only) through Christ who strengthened him. (see Philippians 4:13)

Though he claimed to be the least of all the apostles, he too felt like his journey to Salvation (the promise of eternal life through Christ) was nothing short of a rough one. Amid every trial, re-member this: Blessed is the man that endureth temptation: for when he is tried, he shall receive the crown of life, which the Lord hath promised to them that love him. (See James 1:12, KJV) And we know that all things work together for good to them that love God, to them who are the called according to his purpose. (See Romans 8:28, KJV)

There will be times when you will fail your test. There will be times when you will feel like giving up and running away. There will even be times that you'll repeat your test until you get it right- but you must pass the test. When you cross your red sea and face your giants, don't murmur. When you are at rope's end, don't complain. When you're betrayed by those closest to you, keep going. Do not allow a lack of faith and ingratitude to cause you to fail your test. David had to pass the test. Abraham had to pass the test. Daniel had to pass the test. Esther had to pass the test. Jacob had to pass the test. Job had to pass the test. Now YOU have to pass the test!

Be encouraged; your test is not in vain. Your trial is not to harm you but to promote you. No matter what you go through, God will grant you a reward if you remain faithful. After you've been through it all, God's promise will remain.

There's value in your promise.

On our way from school, we would kick stones, dust, empty plastic bottles, and boxes; you name it. Once your foot could move any object, the front of your shoes would know it. Eventually, that pair of shoes would deteriorate because of all the damage caused by kicking things, and maybe you got a proper spanking or warning for it. Children do silly things. But children don't understand what it means to put in a couple of hours to earn money to buy the shoes they use to kick rubble. They quickly destroy a good pair of shoes without knowing it, and their parents will have to replace it. When they become adults, that is when they realize how much work they'd have to put in to buy a pair of shoes.

Similarly, when God gives you the promise just like that, you'll treat it lightly- you will treat it like the pair of shoes you used to kick stones. You will only learn to appreciate your blessing when you know what you have been through to get it. When you put in the work to receive your promised, then you'll honour it. A saying goes: 'Once you carry your water, you'll learn the value of every drop,' that means, when you know what it feels like to work and earn what you have, you'll appreciate it more. God doesn't want you to obtain a promise that will quickly be of no great value to you- all because you did not put in any work. God is not unjust that He'd demand your sweat, blood, and tears; all He wants is for you to appreciate the value in what He has promised you.

CHOOSE TO OBEY

Deuteronomy 28:15, KJV

But it shall come to pass, if thou wilt not hearken unto the voice of the Lord thy God, to observe to do all his commandments and his statutes which I command thee this day; that all these curses shall come upon thee, and overtake thee:

> Adam and Eve chose to walk away from God's promises when they ate from the tree, fruit of the knowledge of good and evil and were banished from the garden to live under a curse. Hence, they had to work for what they needed as they could eat only through hard labour (see Genesis 3:19). They were given dominion over all that God had made, yet they gave that up for their own will and lived a cursed life until Jesus Christ reversed that curse through His '*Perfect Obedience*'.

When you walk away from God's presence, you walk away from His promises, and you'll run the risk of living under a curse. A life lived in sin epitomizes the powerlessness you will suffer if you walk out of God's provision for your life, and away from His promises. Hence, anything short of God's provision is accursed. Disobedience leads to sin, and sin leads to death. However, perfect obedience has the power to reverse such a curse and keep you in line with God's will for your life, and this positions you to receive His promises so you can live your best life (see Deuteronomy 28:1-14).

How do you live your best life?

The answer to this is by trusting God and living by God's word. It's not always simple or easy, but it is possible. Whatever God has called you to do, He has already approved it. Anyone can live their best life by bearing these principles in mind: loving God with all your heart, soul, and might; loving your neighbour the way you would love yourself, and seek God before anything or anyone else.

What happens when you follow God's law?

When you follow God's law, you are giving up your will to live by His. When you are in total submission to God, you will always be blessed. God honours a man/ woman who accepts His law. God lifts us those who will exalt Him with their obedience. Wherever God leads, He always provides. Your store basket will never go empty, and He will not withhold anything good from you.

What happens when you don't follow God's law?

You need God's guidance and direction in every area of your life. If you fail to trust the author and finisher of your faith, you fail to live. Failure is inevitable if you choose to live your life without

God. Take Romans chapter 1; for example, there was a loss, regret, confusion (reprobate mind-set), conflict, pain, and disaster, which later resulted in indiscipline that and punishment. God's timing isn't the same as yours. God's plan is higher than your opinion, and God's laws far outweigh man's logic.

God's instructions are in His word. Consult Him in prayer and apply His Word to your life; that's how you'll navigate through life's ups and downs. When you take heed to the word of God, it means you're obeying His divine instruction.

Will You Choose To Obey or To Disobey?

Obedience is the key to the peace of God in your life and the blessing you deserve. Proverbs 10:22 says The blessing of the Lord, it maketh rich, and he addeth no sorrow with it. The grace of God brings peace and joy; there is satisfaction for your mind, body, and soul, and there is no regret or loss attached to it. Do you know the cost of disobedience? It will cost you your whole life. God's will is for His children to be obedient to Him.

Even though God made you a promise, you are still required to obey His instructions to obtain the promised and more. God always gives more than He promises (only if you follow Him). Whatever God has promised, you will pass down to many generations because your promise and blessing are not just for you to inherit. The inheritance depends on your obedience to God. If you fall short (are found disobedient or outside of the will of God), then you will not receive your promise or your blessing. Instead, you will receive a curse, and that curse passes down to the next generation as well. God gave you His word, and that's enough proof that He has not called you out to do things on your own.

"All the commandments *[instructions]* which I command thee this day shall ye observe to do *[obey me]*, that ye may live, and multiply, and go in and possess the land *[promise]* which the LORD sware unto your fathers." (See Deuteronomy 8:1 KJV) *[emphasis added]*

We live, flourish, and extend our days through obedience to God, so let your obedience activate your promise (see Deuteronomy 5:33).

By humility and the fear of the LORD are riches, and honour, and life. (See Proverbs 22:4) I.e. you gain health, wealth and long life through your obedience to God.

If you feel like turning your back on God because His promises to you seem impossible, and you've been waiting, and waiting, and waiting, and the light of hope grows dim, I charge you today, the way Paul did, by the mercies of God, to hold fast to God's unchanging hands. Remain confident in God. Do not throw in the towel. Do not let go- even when your hands get weak. Protect your promise, pass the test, and you shall surely reap the reward that awaits you on the other side of your obedience. Remember the days when you had just met God- that encounter that had your heart singing all day and through the nights. That encounter with God that made you feel so much strength; it was as if nothing in this world could discourage you. Take heart, my brother, my sister, in knowing that the same God who met you back then feels the same way about you even now. Come back to the heart of worship. Rekindle that flame for God and love Him even in your tests and trials. Keep fanning your flame, that's how you'll maintain your fire. Remember God's word, and they will help you go through. Fasting and prayer will surely bring back your flame. Keep on believing in God, and He will see you through. God has promised to bless you abundantly, so do not give up now. (see Galatians 6:9) Your troubles and frustrations are only for a season; they cannot compare to what God has in store for you if you hold on. (see Romans 8:18)

There are consequences for giving up on God, which are not for His children to bear. "Therefore, my beloved brethren, be ye steadfast, unmoveable, always abounding in the work of the Lord, forasmuch as ye know that your labour is not in vain in the Lord." (see 1 Corinthians 15:58, KJV)

Deuteronomy 28:1-14 outlines all the beautiful blessings God has to offer. It is up to you to choose between the blessings and the curses. The blessing is the reward that God will give to you if you love Him, trust Him and obey Him only. If you want to obtain God's beautiful promises, you must believe His word. If you want a life of meaning, follow His word.

Deuteronomy 28:15-68 outlines all the blessings that you miss out on if you do not follow God's word. Without His promises, you have no hope, future, and you'll have no peace.

Now, run with haste to obey the Lord's command, and you will receive all that He has promised you.

LET US PRAY...

Father, I thank you for giving me a chance to receive Your promise. Thank you for committing to Your promise to me. Thank you for helping me to see that You only want the best for me because I am your child.

I don't mean to disobey or insult You the way I do. I've put a lot before You many times, and I've walked away from Your presence and provision for me, not knowing I'd suffer harsh consequences, and I'm sorry.

Forgive me for not following Your divine instructions and for walking away from Your promise. Forgive me for ever doubting what You said. Forgive me for looking back. Forgive me for murmuring, complaining, and for interfering in your work by making a mess of everything. I didn't know. You never needed my help. Forgive me for my lack of confidence, love and faith in You.

Deliver me from the destruction of my disobedience!

Deliver me from the doubts that keep me from Your truth!

Deliver me from ingratitude that causes me to murmur and complain!

Deliver me from my ignorance or else I'll perish!

Deliver me from fear, so Your Spirit may dwell in me!

From now on, I'll do my best to honour Your promise to with my faith and obedience. Give me the strength to hold on to what You said, even when I feel like turning back. God, give me the courage to face my tests in full assurance that You will deliver me. I cannot live my best life without You, so I am trusting you to finish this race with me.

These and other mercies I ask You, Lord, in Jesus' name.

Amen.

CONCLUSION

Your faith and obedience to God form a correlation that qualifies you to obtain His promise. Living a life of fruitfulness and fulfilment falls under one condition- YOUR OBEDIENCE. The act of obedience is the premise that determines the fruit you will bear after God's fulfils His will in your life. God pulls you into your destiny to produce, perform, and demonstrate Who He is to you and who you are in Him, and it doesn't get better than that. You must always seek to do what God says so that you will live in God's favour. You cannot go wrong when you obey God. Your obedience to God will develop His character in of you, and give you access to His promise of grace and peace.

When Jesus taught the disciples to pray in Matthew 6:9-13, it was not just any old ordinary prayer. He was teaching them how to obtain the promise. Jesus taught the disciples saying, "Our Father which art in Heaven ... Thy will be done on earth. Give us this day our daily bread ..." This prayer is evidence that after you've done the will of your Heavenly Father on earth, you will receive the bread to sustain you. The scripture also affirms that after you've done the will of God, He will forgive you of your sins and trespasses (even as you forgive others); He will deliver you from all evil (keep you out of harm's way), and make a way of escape (through grace) whenever you face trouble.

God promises joy, everlasting life, abundance, liberty, perfect peace, wisdom, safety and security, excellence in all you do, and good health. You will be blessed because you have the Lord with you, and He never stops keeping His promises. Believe God when He says, He that has begun a good work in you shall surely see it to the end. You have nothing to lose. Let God's perfect will be done in you.